Presented to:

....

On the occasion of:

....

Published in Nashville, Tennessee, by Thomas Nelson®. Thomas Nelson is a registered trademark of Thomas Nelson, Inc.

Good Morning, Lord devotionals were adapted from the following books by Sheila: *Let Go, Get Off Your Knees and Pray, Life Is Tough But God Is Faithful, Infinite Grace, Amazing Freedom,* and *Laugh Out Loud*

Managing Editor: Lisa Stilwell

Text Editor: Lisa Guest

Cover design by AIM Design, Franklin, TN

Page design: Walter Petrie

Thomas Nelson, Inc., titles may be purchased in bulk for educational, business, fund-raising, or sales promotional use. For information, please e-mail SpecialMarkets@ThomasNelson.com.

ISBN 978-1-4041-8960-7

Printed in China

10 11 12 13 14 RRD 5 4 3 2 1

www.thomasnelson.com

Good Morning, Lord

Sheila Walsh

A Division of Thomas Nelson Publishers
Since 1798

ALARM CLOCK. DO THOSE TWO words strike fear in your heart? That annoying noise! That enemy of treasured sleep!

Or are you one who doesn't need technology to help you start your day? You're up before both the sun and the birds, overflowing with immeasurable energy and unquenchable joy as the day begins.

Whether or not you're a morning person, your day has to start sometime, and this little book is a simple encouragement that you start the day with the Lord. If you spend a few minutes reading his Word, acknowledging his presence with you in prayer, being reminded of the big-picture perspective of why it was worthwhile getting up (he loves you and wants to share this day with you!)—your day will go better. Spending some time with your heavenly Father will help you cope with the newspaper headlines, the petty annoyances of the day, and everything in between.

You may be a crack-of-dawn or a crack-of-noon person by nature. Either way, your heavenly Father wants to hear you say, "Good morning!" And you'll never regret starting your day with him.

So grab your Bible, a cup of coffee, and *Good Morning, Lord*—and our Lord, who is good all the time, will help your day get off to a good start!

Love,
Sheila

Today I will look for evidence that you are in everything I encounter.

CHARLES FINNEY ONCE SAID, "A state of mind that sees God in everything is evidence of growth in grace and a thankful heart."* *Everything*. Mr. Finney doesn't offer fine print or exclusions. *Everything*. Consider your life right this second. Do you easily see the hand of God in everything that is happening right now? What, for instance, are you dealing with right now that you don't remember signing up for? Life's harsh intruders often make it hard for us to recognize the truth that our God is always present with us.

But you may be like me. Usually I know enough when a crisis hits to turn to God for strength, grace, and guidance. It's the small stuff that gets me, those moments when my plans are messed up. Those are the times I must learn again to trust God. It's hard for me, because it means I have to let go of my agenda. As I look back over my life, I can think of many times when my plans seemed to fall apart. I see now that God's grace was right there, available, every single time, but sometimes I didn't reach out and receive it. To have my hands free to receive God's grace, I have to be willing to let go of whatever I'm clinging to.

When do you find it easier to turn to God—when you're suddenly facing a huge crisis or as you deal with the small, daily stuff of life? Why do you think that is?

2/23 WHEN SUDDENLY FACING A HUGE CRISIS, BECAUSE GOD CAN BE SOOTHING AND LESSEN THE ANXIETY THAT OCCURS. I AM SELFISH AND USUALLY CRY OUT FOR GOD IN TIMES OF NEED.

I NEED GOD AND I FEEL HIM BEST WHEN TROUBLE COMES, THEN MIRACULOUSLY DISSAPATES.

Think back on a time when your carefully laid plans seemed to fall apart. In what ways was God's grace available to you in that situation?

I THINK ABOUT EVENTS AT ATHPE WITH THE CHURCH. THE GAMEPLAN IS OFTEN ALTERED BY OTHERS ACTIONS, I ALWAYS FEEL FOR THE WORSE. GOD CAUSES THE ALTERATIONS, AND IT ALWAYS WORKS FOR THE BEST

> *Omnipresent, omnipotent God, how wonderful it would be to see you in everything! Continue to grow me toward that end, that I may live with gratitude, especially for the grace of your unfailing love for me and your constant presence with me.*

> Trust in the LORD with all your heart,
> And lean not on your own understanding;
> In all your ways acknowledge Him,
> And He shall direct your paths.
> —PROVERBS 3:5–6

---

* Charles Finney, quoted in Edythe Draper, *Draper's Book of Quotations for the Christian World* (Wheaton, IL: Tyndale, 1992).

Today I will rest in the truth that you are always watching over me.

I LIKE CATS, BUT FORTY-THREE are about forty-two cats too many for me. But forty-three is what my hostess in Bristol, England, had when I stayed with her one night after an evangelistic meeting. I drank my cup of cocoa (despite the cat fur floating in it), thanked my hostess, and headed for bed. "My little darlings will follow you!" she sang out after me. "Your room is where my darlings sleep, too!"

The next morning I woke with a start. I was suffocating! I must be in a cave, a tunnel, I was drowning. . . . No, it was worse than that. "Help, Lord, there's a cat on my face!"

With all my years of traveling, I've slept in some strange places. My great comfort is that the Lord never sleeps. In fact, he watches over me whether I'm in Bangkok, Britain, or Boise, Idaho. And I don't know about you, but that truth is good for me to know. Is it ever hard for you to close your eyes at night? Do you worry about what tomorrow will hold or if you will be safe until morning? Remember this: God never closes his eyes. He is always watching over you . . . even when you have cat fur in your cocoa.

When have you clearly, beyond a shadow of a doubt, known the Lord's protection? Tell of a time when you were very aware that he preserved you from evil.

2/24

DRIVING JOHN HOME AFTER PRACTICE, WE HAD BEEN DRINKING, AND
WE SHOULD NOT HAVE ESCAPED THE COLLISION ON LEICESTER. I HAD

AN ARGUMENT WITH DWAYNE AND LEFT, DWAYNE AND CO. VIOLENTLY ATTACKED BUBBLES, IF NOT FOR GODS INTERVENTION ... I WOULD HAVE JOINED.

Let's be honest. Is there a time in your life when you could make a good argument that the Lord was napping? Talk to him honestly about the pain and repercussions of that experience—and listen for him to reveal how he was, in fact, watching over you.

HURTING MELODY AND THE AFTERMATH ... TWO YEARS OF SELF DESTRUCTION, SHAME, UNFORGIVENESS, TEARS.
— GOD IS GOOD ... PROVIDING CHURCH, WORSHIP, A CALLING, AND WILLOW!

I believe, Lord, that you are always watching over me and that you preserve me from all evil. I believe; help my unbelief.

He will not allow your foot to be moved;
    He who keeps you will not slumber.
Behold, He who keeps Israel
    Shall neither slumber nor sleep. . . .
The LORD shall preserve you from all evil;
    He shall preserve your soul.

—PSALM 121:3–4, 7

Today I will follow Jesus.

IF WE SAY WE'RE WILLING to follow Jesus, what do we mean? I believe there is only one valid reason for following Jesus: because he is worth it. And he is worth it because of who he is in all his love, his understanding, his compassion. Following him means doing so with no strings attached; it means not telling God, "I'll do this if you come through with that." Either Jesus is worth hanging onto in hard times only because he is Jesus, or he is worth nothing. When life doesn't make sense anymore, we can give up, or we can remember who Jesus really is and that, no matter how dark it gets, he is worth it all.

As you've undoubtedly experienced, we may not get an explanation as to why certain things happen—why the dark times are as dark and persistent as they are—but living our lives with certain things unresolved is what faith is all about. For years I drank deeply of the false belief that if only I had enough faith, everything would go my way. But that is simply not true, and so many people are caught and lives are wrecked in the wake of this teaching. "Why is this happening to me? What did I do wrong?" we cry. Heaven cries back, "You've done everything wrong, but I love you anyway. Always have, always will."

When have you been able to extend love to a family member or friend who had done something sinful or hurtful? Be specific about your thoughts and feelings, about your interaction with the person involved, and about how your love was received.

....

....

....

....

....

When has someone shown love for you despite your sin that impacted him/her, your hurtful words, or your thoughtless ways? What did that experience teach you about God's love for you—and about the kind of love we, his people, are to have for others?

....

....

....

....

Lord God, I have made so many mistakes, but you love me anyway! That's wonderful and wondrous news! May I respond by living confident in your love for me and generous in sharing your love with others.

I am convinced that nothing can ever separate us from God's love. Neither death nor life, neither angels nor demons, neither our fears for today nor our worries about tomorrow—not even the powers of hell can separate us from God's love. No power in the sky above or in the earth below—indeed, nothing in all creation will ever be able to separate us from the love of God that is revealed in Christ Jesus our Lord.

—ROMANS 8:38–39 NLT

2/26/11

Today I will listen for your voice directly and not rely solely on what someone else has heard you say.

I LOVE TO READ GOOD Christian books. I enjoy attending events where I have the opportunity to hear speakers talk about their experiences with God or teach on a particular passage. But it's not enough to know what someone else is learning from God, as encouraging as such times may be. I need to be learning and growing too, and such growth happens directly and personally. God talks to his people—to each one of us—through his Word, through the counsel of godly friends, and through the Holy Spirit.

Yet—and you don't need me to tell you this—it takes deliberate and continuous effort to carve out time in our overfull schedules to listen to the voice of God. I am not at all suggesting that we reject godly counsel from those we trust and respect. One of the ways God speaks to us is through the wise counsel of other believers. But God loves one-on-one conversation. Will you take him up on that invitation? He'd love to talk!

When have you been especially encouraged or helped by a godly friend's counsel?

....

....

....

....

....

....

What are some specific steps you can take to help ensure that a
conversation with Jesus, where you have time to listen, happens regularly?

....

....

....

....

....

....

*Lord God, I long to hear your voice but not just secondhand
through teachers, as wonderful and godly as they can be. I long
to hear your voice firsthand. Enable me to intentionally carve
out time in my schedule to listen to your voice—and then,
Lord, to recognize and obey it.*

I am the good shepherd; I know my own sheep, and they know
me, just as my Father knows me and I know the Father. . . . I have
other sheep, too, that are not in this sheepfold. I must bring them
also. They will listen to my voice, and there will be one flock with
one shepherd.

—JESUS IN JOHN 10:14–16 NLT

Today I will practice keeping my mind "stayed on you."

GOD LOVES TO GIVE US the perfect verse from his life-giving Word at the perfect time. After the death of his beloved wife, for instance, Pat opened his Bible and read of a God who promised peace in the midst of turmoil and joy in the deepest sorrow. At first Pat's hopelessness made him feel is if he were losing his mind, and he asked God to hold on to him. But as he kept his mind on God's Word and on the promises he read there, peace began to edge out despair. He read, "You will keep him in perfect peace, / Whose mind is stayed on You" (Isaiah 26:3). Pat asked God to strip him of the lies and half-truths Satan loves to whisper in our ears so that his mind would be focused on the one true God.

Perfect peace is translated from the Hebrew *shalom shalom*, which means "fulfillment, abundance, well-being, security." The phrase *whose mind is stayed on You* comes from two Hebrew words: the first meaning "will, imagination"; the second, "dependent, supported, firm." When our wills and imaginations are dependent on God, when we choose to turn our thoughts to him, we learn the simple truth that God is enough. We find out, as Isaiah wrote, that "in the LORD . . . is everlasting strength" (26:4), and in God's strength we discover fulfillment and security.

What keeps you—your will and imagination—from being entirely dependent on God?

....

....

....

....

When, if ever, have you experienced for yourself the simple and soul-satisfying truth that God is enough? Why don't we believers experience that more regularly?

....

....

....

....

....

Holy God, you know before I tell you how easily distracted I am. As the old hymn says, my heart is prone to wandering, and my thoughts wander too. Yet you alone offer fulfillment, abundance, security—and that's just the beginning of a long list of the blessings I find in you. Teach me to live focused on you.

You will keep in perfect peace
    all who trust in you,
    all whose thoughts are fixed on you!
Trust in the LORD always,
    for the LORD GOD is the eternal Rock.

—ISAIAH 26:3–4 NLT

Today I will praise you for your amazing grace!

HE WAS A CRIMINAL SENTENCED to execution, to being crucified on a cross, the most brutal punishment Rome had devised. Yet whatever wrong choices this man had made in life, with his final breaths he made the only choice that eternally matters. He recognized that the Man hanging next to him was Messiah, King of kings. And this scene from Calvary offers a vivid picture of grace.

When we speak of grace, we define it as unmerited favor, yet so often we feel as if somehow we should measure up to this gift. In the life of this man hanging on a cross, the true meaning of grace becomes abundantly clear. There was not one thing that criminal could do to live a life worthy of Jesus' invitation other than open his heart to the love of God. There was not one deed he could do as a last-minute "Thank you!" All he could do was accept Jesus' gift. That is grace. And, yes, grace can be unfair. Say the criminal's brother lived a life of total devotion to God, honoring the Almighty in every way he knew possible. The grace extended to him would be the same as the grace extended to the brother who had wasted his life. No, it's not fair. It's grace.

In what ways are you still trying to measure up to God's gift of grace? If you're not sure, someone who knows you well might be able to help you answer this question.

2/28

....

....

....

....

....

When did you first accept God's grace? Being able to tell your story helps
others come to accept God's grace as well.

....

....

....

....

....

....

*Father, I am grateful that your grace isn't about getting what's
fair! Your grace is all about your heart, not our hard work or
good behavior. The truth is, no matter what I do or how much
I try, I could never deserve your gift of salvation. Thank you
for looking beyond what is fair and sending your Son to die in
my place so you could extend to me your gift of eternal grace.*

Then [the criminal] said, "Jesus, remember me when
you enter your kingdom." [Jesus] said, "Don't worry, I
will. Today you will join me in paradise."

—LUKE 23:42–43 MSG

Today I will let your light shine into my hidden places.

LET ME INTRODUCE YOU TO someone you probably have something in common with, and you may even have met her before. I'm talking about the Samaritan woman whom Jesus spoke with at the well (John 4). Stopping for water as he walked the dusty roads of Palestine, Jesus let his light shine into her hidden places when he said, "Go and get your husband." This lonely, beaten-down woman realized her hiding was over: "Sir, I don't have a husband." Looking at her and seeing all her sin and guilt, Jesus nevertheless loved her: "I know. You've had five husbands, and you're not married to the man you're living with now." At that point she could choose to have the painful, healing light of God's love set her free.

I'm guessing that you're not standing at a well reading this little book, but I'm pretty certain that you have a hidden place or two. Will you do what the Samaritan woman did? Will you speak the truth—the ugly, sinful truth—that you've hidden away in the darkness of shame and guilt? Will you let the painful, healing love of God shine into that hiddenness and set you free? I have had to do that. I have had to acknowledge the pain at my father's death, pain I had buried deep inside for several years. God washed away the fear and guilt that had festered within me since I was four years old. I could walk away from the past and concentrate on what God was going to do with my future, because I allowed his love to set me free.

What experiences, memories, and/or emotions have you hidden away deep in your mind and heart? If nothing comes to mind, spend some quiet minutes with your loving God and ask him to show you what he wants to set you free of.

....

....

....

What thoughts and emotions surface when you consider that God wants to "do a new thing" (Isaiah 43:19) in your life? Take those to him in prayer and listen for him to respond.

....

....

....

Lord, I am choosing to rest in your sovereignty. You are sovereign over my past: you can and will heal and redeem it. I'm also choosing to trust your sovereignty over my future, anticipating what new thing you want to do in my life. And may I acknowledge your sovereignty in the day-to-day present so that I may live in your light, freed by your love.

The LORD says, "Forget what happened before,
and do not think about the past.
Look at the new thing I am going to do.
It is already happening. Don't you see it?"
—ISAIAH 43:18–19 NCV

Today I will remember that my failure to forgive myself is a prideful choice to not receive your grace.

ONE OF THE GREATEST SAINTS in Christian history began as one of its greatest persecutors—Saul of Tarsus, who became Paul the apostle. We read in Acts 8:3 that, "As for Saul, he made havoc of the church, entering every house, and dragging off men and women, committing them to prison." It was Saul's intent to destroy the church—until, as he traveled the road to Damascus to continue his murderous work there, he met the living Christ. "Saul, Saul, why are you persecuting Me?" was Jesus' very direct question (Acts 9:4), and that question made no sense. As far as Saul was concerned, he wasn't persecuting God but was defending true Judaism. Imagine the shock as Saul recognized his actions for what they were: his misguided killings, the ripple effect on devastated families, and his affront to the Lord of the universe. Imagine the struggle to receive God's forgiveness and to forgive himself. . . .

Paul did receive God's forgiveness and went on to preach powerful sermons—teachings we still read today—about the gift of forgiveness available to all because of Jesus' death on the cross. This forgiveness is a powerful weapon that overcomes the evil in this world and brings healing to our wounded souls, but we must reach out and accept it. To say that we don't deserve to be forgiven is to make our sin more powerful than the blood of Christ. And since God forgives us, we must forgive ourselves. When we refuse, we have made the court of our opinion more powerful than the court of our holy and just God. It must seriously wound the heart of our Father when we will not accept the gift he has given us, the gift of forgiveness that cost him so dearly. After all, our sin was covered by the lifeblood of the Lamb.

What impact does the account of Paul's conversion have on your understanding of forgiveness?

....

....

....

Explain why our inability to forgive ourselves reflects an attitude of pride.

....

....

....

God of the impossible, you got the attention of murderous Saul, changed his heart, and made him a powerful voice for your gospel truth. You also got my attention, and I thank you for the grace of being able to acknowledge Jesus as my Savior and Lord and you as my Father. I ask for the grace to live in the freedom of your forgiveness and love.

If anyone is in Christ, he is a new creation; old things have passed away; behold, all things have become new.

—2 CORINTHIANS 5:17

Today I will consider what it means that you are my friend.

OKAY, WE'LL START WITH A basic truth: Christianity is not an employer-employee contract. Consider Job. Yes, he was God's servant, but even more importantly, he was also God's friend. Throughout Job's entire ordeal, his reactions showed that he did not serve God for what he could get from the Almighty, but for what he could give to the Lord from the very core of his being. Job did not serve God out of fear or duty. He served God out of love, and so it should be between friends.

So be warned! We may run ourselves ragged doing things for God—being a member of every committee at church, attending every prayer meeting, doing whatever job needs to be done—and lose the Lord in the midst of it all. Ultimately, only our loyalty to God as our Friend will hold us when life is tough. And his loyalty to us is the foundation for our loyalty to him. When we blow it, when we fall flat on our face, when we choose our own path for life, there is still a place to go. We can always say to him, "Please hold me tight—and don't let me go!" And because he is my friend, he will always be there to catch me.

What do you think it means to be a friend to God?

....

....

....

....

3/3/11

....

....

What are some specific and practical ways you can be a friend to God in
your daily life?

....

....

....

....

....

....

....

*"What a Friend We Have in Jesus"—it's a classic hymn, but
what does it mean to be your friend, Lord? Please teach me by
the power of your Spirit and the truth of your Word, and then
help me live what I learn.*

You are my friends if you do what I command.
I no longer call you servants,
because a servant does not know his master's business.
Instead, I have called you friends, for everything that I learned
from my Father I have made known to you.

—JESUS IN JOHN 15:14–15 NIV

Today I will focus on being your friend.

"I'M SORRY, SHEILA, BUT YOU'RE going to have to forget this concert tour. You have a growth on your left vocal cord. You not only shouldn't be singing, but you shouldn't even talk for a while." *What?!?* Didn't this doctor—London's finest throat specialist—know that twenty-five thousand tickets had already been sold for the biggest Christian concert tour in Britain's history? How could I tell my manager and road crew that the tour was off? They had spent countless hours putting the tour together, and we were so sure each step of the way that God was guiding and blessing. . . .

Having also been told that he might have to operate if the rest didn't bring healing, I went away to be alone with the Lord for ten days—and for nine of those days I asked God why. I ranted, I raged, I sobbed. When I finally ran out of words, I became aware of a blanket of his love, and I got the distinct impression that God was saying, "Sheila, don't you understand that I love you because of who you are and not for what you do? I don't need you to do things for me. I just really love you." God was teaching me that Christian service is a poor substitute for knowing Jesus. Oh, serving God is important, even vital, but it should never come ahead of realizing that he is first of all our Friend, and without his friendship, life is a meaningless treadmill.

What does Psalm 139 (two verses appear on page 25) reveal about God's intimate love for you?

GOD LOVED ME AT CONCEPTION. GOD CREATED ME, (MIND, BODY, AND SOUL). HIS PURPOSE FOR MY LIFE HAD BEEN

PLANNED FROM THE GET-GO.

What step will you take this week to focus more on becoming God's
friend rather than just running yourself ragged doing something for him?

THIS WEEKEND I WILL ACCEPT GODS PRESENSE EVERYWHERE
I GO, WETHER I AM ACTIVE OR NOT. I WILL TREAT HIM
AS A FRIEND, LAUGHING, ASKING, CRYING, SCREAMING, ECT...
I WILL BE AWARE OF HIS NEEDS AND DISLIKES, AND
I WILL CATOR TO THAT SO TO MAKE GOD AS HAPPY AS
POSSIBLE.

> It's the mystery of grace, Lord—the fact that you love me. I didn't
> do anything to earn your love, and I can't do anything to make
> you love me more or, for that matter, less! Help me receive your
> love and then respond by serving you out of love and gratitude.

For You formed my inward parts;
    You covered me in my mother's womb.
I will praise You, for I am fearfully and wonderfully made;
    Marvelous are Your works,
    And that my soul knows very well.

—PSALM 139:13–14

Today I will slow down enough to notice your fingerprints on your amazing creation.

THE YOUTUBE SERMON BY LOUIE Giglio was amazing. His subject was "The Greatness of God," and the information Louie shared does indeed point to God's greatness. Louie had met a molecular biologist who asked him if he were aware of the existence of a protein molecule in the human body called laminin. (Google it and learn—and see pictures!) Laminin is a cell-adhesive protein molecule that literally holds our human bodies together. The shape of this tiny protein molecule is . . . the shape of a cross. Isn't that amazing? And this tiny form is multiplied many thousands of times over inside our bodies. It can't help but remind us that God is ever-present in our lives—even in the very marrow of our bones!

As if that scientific fact isn't mind-boggling enough, Lana Bateman, our prayer intercessor at Women of Faith, told me about an article by a molecular biologist who is also a brilliant pianist. He wrote that if you take the unique DNA strand that defines each human being and turn it on its side so that it resembles a piano keyboard, every human being has his or her own individual melody. Just think: God has written a song in your very soul. That is as great a mystery to me as the fact that the cross is built into our DNA, and both facts are an overwhelming comfort and a reminder of our Creator's love. Yes, he loves you. It is written into your very DNA.

3|5

What was your initial reaction to today's science facts?

....

....

....

....

....

Reflect on the fact that the very cells that hold your body together are in the shape of a cross. Let the wonder fill you up!

....

....

....

....

Creator God, Father God, I am amazed by the intricacy and complexity of your creation—of the planets in their orbits, of the laminin holding me together, of the seasons we experience, of the relationships you bless us with. May I never lose my sense of wonder at your brilliant creativity and your intricate design in this world, in history, in my body, in my life.

In the beginning God created the heavens and the earth.
—Genesis 1:1

Today I will remember who I am in Christ.

WHEN I WAS SIXTEEN, I stood on the beach of our small fishing town in Scotland and said, "Lord, I'm all yours—but I've nothing to give you. I'm an emotional wreck. I'm afraid of everything. I know I'm ugly. I hate myself, Lord. But if you can do anything with me, I'm yours." I've openly shared my story in different venues through the years; I've talked openly about the path that led to those pain-filled statements about myself and that cry to the Lord. Life's hard times, the sin of others, the fallenness of this world, the messages of the media, the unthinking words of others—so many factors can contribute to a sense of self-loathing. But we don't have to stay in that place. By God's grace, we can learn to embrace the truth of who we are in Christ.

And who are we in Jesus? Better yet, who are *you* in Jesus? Read the following truths slowly so that you hear them with your heart and not just your ears! In fact, trade every *you* for *I* and let the truth penetrate your heart anew! You are cleansed and forgiven (1 John 1:9); you are a new creation (2 Corinthians 5:17). You are loved by your heavenly Father and have been adopted as his child (1 John 3:1). You are fearfully and wonderfully made (Psalm 139:14), and God delights in you (Psalm 147:11). You are God's chosen (1 Peter 2:9); you are the apple of his eye (Psalm 17:8).

What, if anything, keeps you from living with absolute confidence that God loves you and from remembering who you are in Christ?

....

....

....

....

....

Bring out into the light of God's healing and transforming love those
dark experiences that contributed and perhaps continue to contribute to
your struggle to like yourself, your struggle to accept God's love, and to
remember who you are in Christ.

....

....

....

....

....

*Lord, what better place to be reminded of your love than among
your people! Thank you for believers in my life who love me with
your love and who help me believe and remember who I am in
Christ. And, Father, who I am in Jesus is amazing. Thank you
for your indescribable and unfailing love for me.*

You are a chosen generation, a royal priesthood,
a holy nation, His own special people,
that you may proclaim the praises of Him who called
you out of darkness into His marvelous light.

—1 PETER 2:9

Today I will be your student, listening for you to show me when I've mentally and emotionally crossed over from healthy guilt to destructive shame.

GUILT HAS A PURPOSE. IT is there to (hopefully) teach you. It has a point of beginning and ending. Shame, however, is not as clearly defined. It doesn't seem to have a beginning or an end; it just is. . . . Guilt tells me I have done something wrong, and that awareness brings hope. I can ask for forgiveness; I can work to right a wrong I've committed. But shame tells me I *am* something wrong, and there is no hope there. Where do I go to change who I am at my core? How can I fix it? . . . Shame preys on a person like a ravenous, demanding monster that sits in the pit of your stomach, wraps its cold arms around your shoulders, and doesn't let go.

Shame is a devastating sickness of the soul that tells us not to show up. It tells us that we don't belong, that if people knew who we really are, we would be asked to leave. Do you sense the hellish breath of the enemy behind these words? He whispers, *People don't really like you. Everyone can see there is something wrong with you. You don't belong here.* God, however, counters that falsehood with truth: *You are loved. You are worth loving. You are my precious creation, a daughter of the King of kings, yes, a princess in my eternal kingdom. And nothing can ever separate you from my love; nothing you do can make me love you less—or more.* Hear that truth and believe it!

When has guilt served its good purpose in your life?

....

....

....

....

Do you struggle with shame-filled thoughts and feelings? If too many of
your thoughts are tinged or stained with shame, memorize one (or more)
of these passages so that you are using God's Word of truth to combat
the lies: Psalm 139:13–14; Romans 8:38–39; 1 John 3:1.

....

....

....

....

*Creator God, your Word says that when you look down on
me, you have eyes full of love and delight. I believe; help my
unbelief. . . . At times—as you know—it is hard for me to
receive your love. When the voice of shame fills my head and
heart, help me go straight to you for healing and freedom,
hope and truth.*

Keep me as the apple of Your eye.

—PSALM 17:8

Today I will savor the fact that I am your daughter, a princess in the family of the King of kings.

ISN'T IT WONDERFUL THAT SCRIPTURE is full of stories of women who met God and were never the same again? Whether it was Ruth, who found God out of her desire to honor her mother-in-law, or Rahab, who is described in the Bible as a harlot but who recognized the God of Israel as God indeed, God gave these precious women a future. Not only that, but Rahab gave birth to Boaz, who married Ruth. Ruth gave birth to Obed, who was Jesse's father, who in turn was the father of King David. These two women, Rahab and Ruth, are in the lineage of Christ (Matthew 1:5). Clearly, God forgave their past and blessed their future.

How much of your life have you spent looking in the rearview mirror at the story of your life? You may have had an unhappy childhood, an irrational mother, or an indifferent father, and you still feel the wounds deeply. If so, I have great empathy for you. All of us long to know that we are loved and valued, but spending too much time looking at our life in the rearview mirror—looking at what we didn't receive when we were younger—can lead to a wreck.

In what ways are you—like Ruth and Rahab—not the same since meeting God? Be specific.

....

....

....

Spending too much time looking at life in the rearview mirror can definitely lead to a wreck. What fender-bender has resulted in your life because of your concern about those images in the rearview mirror?

....

....

....

....

....

....

Redeemer God, I love how you use the most unlikely people to play key roles in your kingdom work. Lord, you know my story—my weaknesses, my sins, my missteps, my unlikeliness— but I ask you to use me to build your kingdom. And please keep me from wrecks and fender-benders along the way.

We are His workmanship, created in Christ Jesus
for good works, which God prepared beforehand
that we should walk in them.

—EPHESIANS 2:10

Today I will ask you to show me an opportunity to be a good Samaritan.

THE PROMOTER TOLD ME THE site of the concert was not a very safe area, but after the sound check I was desperate for a cup of tea. I rushed down the street, got my tea, and was hurrying back to safety when I noticed a man coming toward me. Clearly, he lived on the streets. His hair was matted and dirty, his clothes were torn and filthy, he didn't have any shoes on his feet, and he had a strange look in his eyes. As the wild-looking man got closer, he asked, "Can you give me something to drink?" I quickly thrust my hot tea into his hands, raced back to my dressing room, and forgot all about him—until I saw him in the crowd that had come up near the stage after the concert.

Two young people had seen the man on the streets and realized that he needed God's love. They stopped, invited him to the concert, bought him a ticket—and a new "Sheila Walsh" sweatshirt—and then celebrated as he walked forward to give his life to Jesus at the close of the concert. These two precious souls then made arrangements to pick him up the next morning at a men's hostel, where he was staying, and take him to church. What opposite reactions to the wild-eyed young man! The man I had seen as threatening and dangerous was perceived by these two young people as someone who needed Jesus, and they reached out to love him.

Read the passage from Luke 10 on the following page. When have you been in need of a good Samaritan? Who passed by? Who, if anyone, stopped? What do you think prompted people to pass by—and what prompted that one person to stop?

CANYONLANDS (MARCUS, JOSH, NATHAN & ME)
WATER CRISIS.

What message does God have for you in this account of the wild-eyed man?

God of all compassion, please keep me from being too busy to
notice and too busy to help someone along my path who has
a need that I could definitely help meet. Please keep me from
being afraid or too self-centered when you want me to act—
and may you be glorified when I obey you.

A certain man went down from Jerusalem to Jericho, and
fell among thieves, who stripped him of his clothing,
wounded him, and departed, leaving him half dead. . . . A certain
Samaritan, as he journeyed, came where he was. And when he
saw him, he had compassion. So he went to him and bandaged
his wounds, pouring on oil and wine; and he set him on his own
animal, brought him to an inn, and took care of him.

—JESUS IN LUKE 10:30, 33–34

John 15:9-17

Today I will choose to trust you rather than fear the very real things there are to fear in this fallen world.

TRUST IS FOUNDATIONAL TO A believer's life, yet I have long been on a journey to understand the connection between fear and trust. I know that at times in my life I have been crippled by fear, but there has always been this strong call inside my spirit: *trust me.* What does it mean to trust? Does it mean that we will never again be afraid, or does it mean that fear will have a part in the play but not be a main character? And what about the promise of Proverbs 3:5–6, "Trust in the LORD with all your heart, / And lean not on your own understanding; / In all your ways acknowledge Him, / And He shall direct your paths"? When I was twelve, I wondered if I were to do things that make no sense to me if I believed that God was leading me. My mom tried to explain that if I honored God in the choices I made, he would keep me on a straight path.

Despite God's promises, despite his infinite power and goodness and love, an element of fear seemed—and seems—reasonable to me. After all, we live in a world of people who use us and abuse us; friends betray us and husbands leave. Furthermore, God in his wisdom and mercy doesn't always stop the evil that makes its way to our door. Evil has walked this earth since the Fall. From Genesis to Revelation, there is a call from God the Father and Christ his Son: *Trust me! Don't be afraid!*

When have you trusted God despite your fear? In what ways did God make his presence with you known?

....

....

....

....

In what current situation are you weighing trust vs. fear?

....

....

....

....

....

Almighty God, you who are my fortress and my strength, you know that I sometimes find myself struggling between trusting you and fearing some very real-life dangers, if not also some very real but imagined possibilities. May I leave my anxiety at the foot of the cross and take steps of faith, empowered by recognition of your Resurrection power.

The LORD is my light and my salvation;
Whom shall I fear?
The LORD is the strength of my life;
Of whom shall I be afraid?

—PSALM 27:1

Today I will extend to others the grace Jesus himself has shown me, looking beyond the outer shell to the heart within.

NO ONE HAD EVER DONE a concert in this small Kansas town, and only fifty people were expected to attend my concert. For whatever reason, forty-nine of the people sat in the back three rows of the church. In the front row one man sat alone—and he never clapped once! I found myself getting annoyed! Even with eye contact from me, he didn't clap! I didn't understand, and I was still trying to figure it out after the concert. As I sat in the pastor's study thinking about the strange behavior, someone suddenly kicked the door. I opened it, and there stood my adversary. Smiling from ear to ear he said, "You will never know how much tonight has meant to me. I have all your albums, and I've asked God for a long time to bring you here." As I looked at this precious, loving man, I realized he had no arms. . . .

The Hebrew word for grace means "to bend, or stoop." Donald Barnhouse, the late pastor and Bible scholar, painted a beautiful picture of grace: "Love that goes upward is worship, love that goes outward is affection, love that stoops is grace." When we didn't deserve it, God stooped down and became a Man. What a picture of grace, the kind of grace he wants us to extend to others. Including people who don't clap when we sing. . . .

What message did God have for you through this devotional?

....

....

....

Who has extended you grace because he or she knew your story
and understood what was behind something you said or did? Who
has extended you grace despite not knowing your story and not
understanding why you acted or spoke in a certain way? Write these
people notes of appreciation.

....

....

....

*Holy God, I am far too quick to judge people and not
consider their story. I am far too slow to extend the kind
of grace you extended to me through the Incarnation,
Crucifixion, and Resurrection, the kind of grace you extend
to me every day. Please forgive me, transform me, and use
me as a conduit of your grace.*

Scarcely for a righteous man will one die; yet perhaps for a good man
someone would even dare to die. But God demonstrates His own love
toward us, in that while we were still sinners, Christ died for us.

—ROMANS 5:7–8

Today I will, by your grace, be aware of when I'm tempted to take the easy way out or to take a situation into my own hands and, by doing either, turn away from you.

THE OFFER WAS STRAIGHTFORWARD. "WORSHIP me," Satan said to Jesus, "and I'll give you all the kingdoms of the world." Jesus declined the offer. Understanding his assignment on this earth, he was not about to accept the crown without the cross. But consider the significance of this temptation. We automatically remind ourselves that Jesus was God's Son and that the plan had always been for him to suffer for our redemption. But Jesus was also fully man, and here Satan proposed an easier path than the one he was walking toward Calvary. Yet Jesus refused to take the easy way out. He refused to worship Satan, an act that would have been an ugly blemish on the spotless Lamb of God. Jesus would no longer have been the perfect fulfillment of God's law, the perfect sacrifice, the means of our salvation. . . .

You and I both know what it's like to be tempted to grab what seems right or necessary or to take an easy way out of the hard work of being a follower of Christ. Most of us want to avoid pain, and it's human nature to want what we can't have. Yet, when we take things into our own hands, we lose the opportunity to allow God to work on our behalf for the greater good. (You might want to read that sentence again!) When we take situations into our own hands, we tend to turn away from God himself. Jesus didn't, though. He looked at everything Satan offered him, looked ahead to the cross and the agony, and chose to follow God.

When have you been tempted to take an easier path rather than the one you believed would honor God?

....

....

....

Describe a time when you resisted the temptation to take things into your own hands. What good did God do on your behalf? In what ways was his plan a greater good than what you could have done in your own power?

....

....

....

Wise and loving Father, forgive me for those times when I long for—and especially for those times when I choose—an easier path than the one you have chosen for me. Forgive me and help me to be more like Jesus: always choosing to follow you, to trust you, to obey you.

If anyone desires to come after Me, let him deny himself, and take up his cross daily, and follow Me.

—Jesus in Luke 9:23

Today I will, by relying on your power, stand strong against my enemy.

ONE OF HIS MOST POPULAR deceptions is that he is an impish little red figure with a mischievous grin, a not-too-threatening pitchfork in his hand, and a tail that ends in a point. But Satan is real and far more powerful than the cartoon image suggests! Our enemy specializes in lies, deceit, confusion, desperation, and depression. As a fallen angel, he is a limited being, but he still has tremendous strength and clever strategies. He moves in to tempt us right at our particular point of need, and he always times his temptations for when we're feeling weak, stressed, desperate, and confused. With God's permission, he throws his worst at us and sits back to see what will happen. God allowed Satan to test Job to see if he really were God's person (Job 1–2), and I think God does that with each of us.

But even when God allows us to experience a season of testing, he doesn't leave us alone or unarmed. We have his promise that he is with us always (Matthew 28:20), and he has also provided us with the armor of God. When we are wearing the belt of God's truth, we recognize Satan's lies. When we have the breastplate of righteousness in place, we are confident of our standing as forgiven and beloved. When we hold up the shield of faith, we "will be able to quench all the fiery darts of the wicked one" (Ephesians 6:16). The helmet of salvation protects our mind from the enemy's lies, God's Word is our sword of protection against deceit and confusion, and, shod with the gospel of peace, we can move forward in confidence and strength. Know that the best-dressed believer wears all these pieces all the time!

When have you been most aware of the very real power of Satan in your life? What did you learn from that experience?

....

....

....

....

What God-blessed and God-protected middle ground do you think a believer is wise to walk?

....

....

....

....

Almighty God, you are indeed almighty—as the Cross clearly illustrates—so I don't need to worry about who ultimately wins the battle that rages between you and Satan. I know, too, that I can trust in your powerful presence with me and in the armor you provide me to help me in my encounters with the enemy. May you be glorified whenever I do battle!

Put on the whole armor of God, that you may be able
to stand against the wiles of the devil.

—EPHESIANS 6:11

Today I will turn to you to find the strength and the path of escape when I encounter temptation.

WHEN YOU HEAR THE PHRASE "immediate felt needs," what do you think of? Me too: food! And that's what Satan thought of when he approached the very hungry Jesus at the end of the forty-day fast in the desert. "If You are the Son of God, command that these stones become bread," Satan said (Matthew 4:3). What a calculated approach by the enemy! Of course Jesus would have been very hungry at the end of forty days without food. And if you have ever allowed yourself to become really hungry, you know that it is much easier to be irritable and—more seriously—not so clearheaded.

So Satan tempts Jesus with something very basic—something we can all understand and appreciate at gut level. I think that's significant, if for nothing else than it shows us how sneaky Satan is. Rather than tempt Jesus with something overtly evil like lust or murder, Satan appealed to what would seem innocent, innocuous. We all need food to live, and Satan was just offering a little something to tide Jesus over. Yet Jesus replied, "It is written, '*Man shall not live by bread alone, but by every word that proceeds from the mouth of God*'" (v. 4). Bread might satisfy for a moment, but to really live we need the Word of God.

What temptations do you face most frequently or find the most difficult to resist?

....

....

....

....

....

....

What does the promise of 1 Corinthians 10:13 (below) reveal about your heavenly Father's plan for your protection and defense?

....

....

....

....

....

> *Almighty and all-wise God, thank you that when you call me to do something—to stand strong against Satan and the temptation he puts in my path—you empower me to do that: you promise to give me both the strength I need to stand strong as well as an escape from the temptation. Thank you!*

No temptation has overtaken you except such as is common to man; but God is faithful, who will not allow you to be tempted beyond what you are able, but with the temptation will also make the way of escape, that you may be able to bear it.

—1 CORINTHIANS 10:13

Today I will marvel at your amazing and unstoppable grace.

As a young man with no strong roots or beliefs, Tex headed to California looking for peace, love, and rock and roll. Instead, he met up with Charles Manson and became part of the infamous Manson family. On August 9, 1969, Tex and other Manson family members broke into the home of actress Sharon Tate (she was just two weeks away from giving birth) and murdered her and four others. Upon his arrest, Tex Watson was sentenced to death. In 1972, however, his death sentence was overturned, and he was sentenced to life in prison.

The nation as a whole was pretty much done with Tex and other Manson family killers, but Tex's praying, believing parents were not. They wrote to several evangelists asking them to visit their son in prison. As a result of one of those visits, Charles "Tex" Watson asked Christ into his life in 1975. Five years later he founded Abounding Love Ministries to minister to prisoners and their families, and in 1983 he became an ordained minister. Clearly, God's grace knows no boundaries. It can flow through prison bars and soften the hardest of hearts.

Think about your own story. What did God do to get your attention and/ or move you to the point of asking Jesus to be your Savior and Lord?

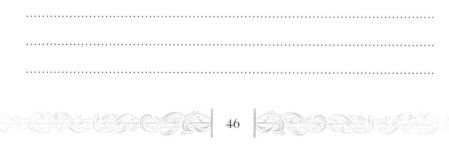

....

....

Who tops your "Least Likely to Be Saved" list right now? Spend a few minutes in prayer for that person. Nothing is impossible for God!

....

....

....

....

....

Lord God, please keep me faithful to pray for those people who seem beyond your reach and impossibly cold and hard-hearted toward you. Forgive my doubts; forgive my laziness in prayer. And know, Lord, that I look forward to celebrating your saving work in the lives of those people.

When he was still a long way off, his father saw him. His heart pounding, he ran out, embraced him, and kissed him. The son started his speech: "Father, I've sinned against God, I've sinned before you; I don't deserve to be called your son ever again." But the father wasn't listening. . . . "My son is here—given up for dead and now alive! Given up for lost and now found!" And they began to have a wonderful time.

—LUKE 15:20–22, 24 MSG

Today as I spend time alone with you, show me what is going on inside me.

THE SUMMER OF 1992 WAS one of the busiest seasons of my life as I juggled being cohost of *The 700 Club*, hosting *Heart to Heart with Sheila Walsh*, flying somewhere to do concerts on Friday and Saturday nights, flying home to Virginia Beach, and starting all over again on Monday mornings. I used to blame my manager for overbooking me, but in retrospect I think I liked the lack of time to think or be alone. Silence was disturbing to me. Silence and solitude invite us to take a look at what might be going on inside, and I didn't want to do that.

Maybe you have felt like that or even feel like that now. Maybe God seems far away and you have the sense that he is not even hearing your prayers, much less answering them. Many vastly different things can contribute to such feelings. We can feel cut off from God if we have chosen a path of destruction rather than the lifestyle set forth in his Word . . . if we are harboring ill will toward someone . . . if we are choosing self-righteousness rather than forgiving someone who hurt us, especially when that person isn't the least bit sorry . . . if we are dealing with illness or depression, insecurity or doubt, the enemy of our souls or the enemy we can be to ourselves. Feelings, however, don't change the fact that God is with us always.

When, if ever and perhaps now, have you found silence or a slower pace threatening because you didn't really want to see or deal with what was going on inside?

....

....

....

....

What does God seem to be nudging you to do in response to this devotional?

....

....

....

Holy God, I come before you—who already knows my heart— to ask you to gently help me know my own heart better. Show me why I am feeling distanced or even cut off from you. Show me, too, your presence with me . . . and where I go from here.

To You I will cry, O LORD my Rock:
    Do not be silent to me,
    Lest, if You are silent to me,
    I become like those who go down to the pit.
Hear the voice of my supplications
    When I cry to You,
    When I lift up my hands toward Your holy sanctuary.

—PSALM 28:1–2

Today I will ask you to help me take a step toward releasing bitterness and extending forgiveness.

HAVE YOU NOTICED—IN YOURSELF OR in others—that the bitter lack of forgiveness can poison a soul and ruin a life? You and I can hold on to that toxic emotion until it's hard for us to know where we end and where the bitter unforgiveness begins. We become hostages to the pain of the past, and that pain can take a toll emotionally, relationally, spiritually, and physically. Yes, physically. That fact, confirmed by twentieth-century doctors, was also discussed long ago in the Torah and other Jewish literature. In those ancient writings, for instance, the gallbladder is thought to be the seat of all diseases. In Hebrew, the word for gallbladder is *marah*, meaning "bitter." The word *marah* is also given a numerical value—*machalah*, meaning "eighty-three." Jewish culture believes that eighty-three illnesses have their source in the gallbladder, which, when stressed by unresolved anger and bitterness, produces too much bile. Think about the last time you were angry and your stomach tightened—a physical reaction. You get the idea.

But forgiving—letting go of the right to get even—can be very hard. After all, it's human nature to want to hurt the one who hurts us. So often we hold on to our unforgiveness because we just can't relinquish the idea of retribution. But God claims vengeance for himself (Deuteronomy 32:35). We can't expect a feel-good ending for all our woes. We simply have to trust that justice will take its God-ordained course.

When have you experienced physical symptoms of a lack of unforgiveness? Why do you think God created us that way?

....

....

....

....

Why does our Creator God, our loving heavenly Father, command us to forgive?

....

....

....

Holy and forgiving God, you know the bitterness and unforgiveness I am holding on to—and I want to be free. Help me let go of my right to get even with the one(s) who hurt me. Help me choose to forgive despite how I feel inside because you command it—and you do so for my good.

We know Him who said,
"Vengeance is Mine, I will repay," says the Lord.
And again, *"The LORD will judge His people."*
It is a fearful thing to fall into the hands of the living God.
—HEBREWS 10:30–31

Today I will take another step toward forgiving someone I've struggled to forgive.

A FRIEND LIED ABOUT ME to my two closest friends, and I could not defend myself without betraying the trust of someone dear to me. Feeling helpless and betrayed, I spent many sleepless nights and wept many bitter tears. But in the midst of it all, I was faced with Christ's command to forgive so that my heavenly Father would forgive me. The Lord is very clear: God will have no mercy on us if we recognize someone else's sin against us and refuse to forgive that person. Remember your own need, Jesus was saying. When we refuse to forgive, we are setting ourselves up as a judge and demanding that others be perfect—something we ourselves can't do. God will judge and demand perfection of us when we judge others.

When we forgive, we see through other people's behavior to their need. We recognize their guilt and at the same time see our own. We realize that we won't find justice in this world—it doesn't live here. So we give up the fruitless, heartbreaking search for it, and we give mercy to those who have wounded us. So I asked God to bless the woman who had wronged me. Only in remembering my own need for forgiveness could I choose to forgive her. I didn't feel like forgiving. I chose to forgive.

Who has probably struggled to forgive and has in fact forgiven you for something you did or said? What, if anything, do you know about that person's struggle? What has his or her forgiveness meant to you?

....

....

....

....

Whom are you struggling to forgive? Why is it significant to you during this struggle that someone has struggled to forgive you and has genuinely forgiven you? Why is it significant that God himself has forgiven you for your sins?

....

....

....

....

God of justice, your Word clearly teaches that you will not forgive my sins if I do not forgive the sins committed against me. Work in my heart, I pray, so that my forgiveness will be genuine, so that I will mean it when I ask you to bless the one who hurt me. I don't want my sin of unforgiveness to block your forgiveness of any of my sin!

For if you forgive men their trespasses, your heavenly Father will also forgive you. But if you do not forgive men their trespasses, neither will your Father forgive your trespasses.

—Jesus in Matthew 6:14–15

Today I will choose to be open with a trusted fellow believer about one of my failures or weaknesses and let God minister to me through that person.

WHAT COMES TO MIND WHEN you hear the word *righteous?* Maybe you think of Jesus himself, the Righteous One. But maybe you think of folks trying to be superhero believers. Do you realize, though, that we become righteous by admitting our weaknesses to one another, not by covering up our sins and weaknesses? Do you know that we gain healing and strength when we allow our brothers and sisters to know us and pray for us?

When we try to become superheroes, we hide our failures, we say nothing about our doubts, we don't confess our sins to one another, and we don't receive prayer from fellow believers. The result of such feigned perfection is loneliness, and we set ourselves up as an easy target for the enemy. Instead, we who name Jesus as our Savior and Lord must be willing to admit our needs, but so often we feel obliged to grin like Cheshire cats so we will be "good witnesses." This pretense results in isolation from God and one another, not Christian community; stagnation, not spiritual growth; staying stuck, not experiencing freedom in Christ.

What, if anything, keeps you from being open and honest about your faults and weaknesses?

....

....

....

....

Have you ever heard someone confess sin publicly, perhaps just in front
of you but maybe before a large group? What was your reaction to that
person? Does your reaction encourage you to be genuine and vulnerable
like that? Explain.

....

....

....

....

....

*Creator God, you know best what is good for us, and you call
me to confess my sin, to be open with fellow believers. Please
help me do so for my good, for the sake of community, for
protection from the enemy, and for your glory.*

**Confess your trespasses to one another,
and pray for one another, that you may be healed.
The effective, fervent prayer of a righteous man avails much.**
—JAMES 5:16

Today I will meditate on your amazing, infinite, and unconditional love for me.

WHEN WE FEEL WE ARE not valued or treasured—and the bumps and bruises of life can definitely contribute to such feelings—we tend to withdraw out of hurt. But there is another way to live, and that involves trusting in God's love. His love is never conditional. He doesn't wait to see what we do or how we behave before deciding whether or not to love us. And he never looks at us and thinks that we need to lose ten pounds or would look better as a brunette. Instead, God sees each one of us as a priceless, beautiful treasure. He never runs out of love or withholds his love from us. I believe if we could hold this truth deep in our hearts, it would set us free to love others.

After all, what woman doesn't want the solid, unshakable knowledge that she is loved, significant, cherished, priceless? Human romance is wonderful, but it comes and goes. God's passionate love for us, however, never wanes. It is my prayer for you this day that God, by his grace, will help you understand more fully the depth, height, and measure of his love for you so that you will be free to love and to love deeply.

Who in your life offers or has offered you conditional love . . . has seemingly run out of love for you . . . or has withheld love from you? Pray for those people because their own hurt is undoubtedly at the root of their hurtful behavior toward you. Ask the Lord to help you forgive them and to enable you to love them—perhaps only from afar—with his gracious love.

....

....

....

....

....

Which statement in today's devotional do you find most life-giving and hope-filled? Spend a few minutes thanking God for his love and asking him to help you embrace it more wholeheartedly.

....

....

....

....

....

Father, help me truly believe today that you see me as a beautiful, priceless treasure. Thank you for your passionate, unconditional love for me.

May [you] be able to comprehend with all the saints what is the width and length and depth and height— to know the love of Christ which passes knowledge.

—EPHESIANS 3:18–19

Today I will embrace my identity as a follower, a disciple of Jesus Christ.

WHAT MOTHER COULD BEAR TO see her son nailed to a cross, mocked and tortured, executed in such a barbaric way? What had Mary's trust in God gained her? . . . The next time we hear Mary's name, she is one of the crowd in the Upper Room, just before the Holy Spirit fell on them all (Acts 1:14). We see her as a disciple and follower of Christ the Messiah and Savior. Yes, Mary has lost her husband and watched men torture and kill her firstborn son; she knows pain and loss. Yet we see her acting in trust as a disciple of Jesus Christ.

What an encouragement Mary's example is! Her experience means that wherever you are in your life right now, the joy and purpose that Mary knew are within your grasp. You see, Mary discovered a calling on her life that was far greater than her calling as a wife or a mother. It was the calling to be a follower of her son, Jesus, the Christ. She let go of what she cherished more than her own life to embrace that higher calling. I do not for one moment want to minimize the pain of what your life has brought you or what might come. But I want to remind you that there is a Rock we have been invited to build our lives on, and this Rock cannot be shaken. Bottom line, we are loved by the One who is love. We are loved by the One who has overcome the enemy. We are loved by the One who says, *Trust me.*

What new appreciation for Mary do you have after reading this devotional?

....

....

....

....

....

....

What evidence could someone find in your life that you are following a calling higher than career, motherhood, marriage, or anything else?

....

....

....

....

....

....

Almighty God, I simply want to follow Jesus. You know the things that interfere—my sin, my wandering heart, my easily distracted mind as well as responsibilities as wife, mother, church work, and career. And just living—the housework, the laundry, the shopping, the cooking—takes so much time and energy. Teach me to follow Jesus despite and in the midst of all this.

Seek first the kingdom of God and His righteousness.
—JESUS IN MATTHEW 6:33

Today I will try to be aware of ways I'm still trying to earn your love. I want to learn to rest in your grace.

"CHRISTIAN, GOD'S LOVE FOR US is not based on our behavior. It's based on his heart and his character. That's grace." As I've watched my son grow in his understanding of grace, the greatest obstacle for him—and for all of us!—has been the way he often connects God's favor to his behavior. It just makes too much sense that when we do good things, God applauds our righteous behavior, and when we slip up and fall, he frowns on us. But God is not a Scout leader or an etiquette coach. His love is lavish and immeasurable and, to be honest, quite difficult for us mere humans to get our hearts and minds around. And I'll gladly share my theory as to why that's the case.

Simply put, I think there is just something in us human beings that wants to feel that we have contributed in some way to whatever we receive. When it comes to the grace of God, however, we contribute nothing. Absolutely nothing—and that's hard for us to swallow. We know we don't bring as much to the table as God does, but we want to feel as if we've done our bit for the team! Again, when it comes to the grace of God, we contribute absolutely nothing.

When and how were you first introduced to God's grace? In what ways was that moment, in and of itself, a moment of grace?

....

....

....

....

....

Why do you struggle to receive and/or rest in God's grace?

....

....

....

....

....

> *Amazing Lord, the Giver of amazing grace, I am humbled by your love. I don't bring anything to the table when it comes to my salvation. I don't do anything for the team when it comes to being forgiven and accepted as your child. My redemption is based on your heart and your character; it's all about you and only you. I love you.*

Everyone has sinned and fallen short of God's glorious standard, and all need to be made right with God by his grace, which is a free gift. [We] need to be made free from sin through Jesus Christ. God sent him to die in our place to take away our sins. We receive forgiveness through faith in the blood of Jesus' death.

—ROMANS 3:23–25 NCV

Today I will thank you for your love when I'm tempted to ask for answers instead.

Maybe you have a friend like Debbie in your life, a friend living with a death sentence. In Debbie's case, the enemy is multiple sclerosis. And maybe you're like me: you can accept your friend's inevitable death. You believe, as I do, that "to be absent from the body . . . [is] to be present with the Lord" (2 Corinthians 5:8). But you struggle to accept the suffering your friend must endure before death. Why must our friend suffer so much now? If God isn't going to heal our friends, why won't he just take them home where they will no longer hurt! One time when I had that thought, God took me to Romans 8:36–37 (see page 63). I read those words of the apostle Paul and thought, *Debbie isn't being a conqueror. She is being conquered daily!* But I needed to reconsider what conquering really is.

Conquerors are satisfied to know that God loves them. Pain and death may destroy their bodies, but they know their souls will live forever because of God's love. With that knowledge, these conquerors can live with unanswered questions. They don't confine God to a box of neatly packaged answers. They are able to depend on God without demanding explanations from him. Pain and death have not destroyed Debbie's love for Jesus, and her faith in God's love for her keeps her faithful to him. And I know she will remain faithful until she is with God in heaven.

What conqueror are you privileged to know or even know about? Write about what that person has taught you or helped you understand.

....

....

....

....

Why would you rather have God's love than answers to hard questions about life's pain and loss?

....

....

....

....

Lord God, forgive me for wanting answers instead of being satisfied with your unchanging love for me. After all, no explanation could be as solid a foundation for life or as sure a hope for the future as your love is. Thank you for your love—and, whatever comes my way in this life, may I be a conqueror because of your love.

"For Your sake we are killed all day long;
We are accounted as sheep for the slaughter."
Yet in all these things we are more than conquerors through Him who loved us.

—ROMANS 8:36–37

Today I will open my eyes to see that you have always been with me, even in the incomprehensibly hard and painful times.

"WHAT SHOULD HAVE HAPPENED DID." That statement was made by Paul "Bear" Bryant, former head football coach at the University of Alabama, when he was asked about a loss against a team they were expected to beat. Applying that to more than a sporting event—to events in my life and in the lives of people I know—made me bristle at first, but then I began to chew on the idea. If we believe that God controls our course in life and has our best intentions at heart as he does so, then "What should have happened did." Add to that the truth that we were never alone, never abandoned. Our omnipresent God says, *My beloved child, I was there. I held you although you could not see my arms. I caught each tear that fell. You were never alone.*

That may be hard to believe if you are dealing with pain from a father who sexually abused you, a husband who is an alcoholic, or a serious issue with a child. You would be justified in asking, "How can you say what should have happened did?" My answer would simply be that being set free from the past means accepting what is true, not mulling over or dwelling on what we wish were true. Now I'm not trying to belittle your situation! But we have to make peace with what was or is if we are going to be able to let go and move forward. So I encourage you to let go of that past—your "what should have been"—and embrace your "what is" and your "what can be." Truth is powerful, at times it is heartbreaking, but ultimately it will deliver you.

What perhaps heartbreaking truth about a formative experience in your past do you need to accept? Be specific—and try to identify how wishing that experience hadn't happened holds you to the past.

....

....

....

Look again at that experience you just identified, but with this truth in mind: *My beloved child, I was there. I held you although you could not see my arms. I caught each tear that fell. You were never alone.* What hope and/or comfort do you find in that truth?

....

....

....

Almighty God, you who knows my story, some of what this devotional says is tough to get my mind and heart around. In these few quiet minutes, please let me feel your love. Help me leave at your feet my questions about my past, especially the "why's." Remind me of your goodness and faithfulness to me so that I may know comfort and hope in you.

You shall know the truth,
and the truth shall make you free.
—JESUS IN JOHN 8:32

Today I will trust you for whatever is happening in my life.

MENTION JONI EARECKSON TADA'S NAME in almost any country in the world, and believers will smile. We all know about the beautiful young athlete whose spinal column was severed in a diving accident. Since that tragic event, Joni has learned to live day in and day out, year after year, with the reality of a broken body. Joni could have given up on God. She could have raged at him for the rest of her life for allowing that horrific accident to happen. She could have listened to Satan's subtle promptings to feel sorry for herself. Instead, she chooses to be a living sacrifice: she chooses every morning to love God and to trust him for one more day.

And so does Kathy Bartalsky, a dear young woman who lost both of her children and her husband. Kathy's sufferings drove her to look long and hard into the face of God to see if he were still a loving God. As she looked and questioned, God showed her a new level of love and gave her a new passion to serve him, no matter the cost. "If we believe in God only for the blessings he can give us," Kathy told me, "our belief in him is not based on love and trust but on our own selfish desires and our own concept of what we think God owes us." Knowing Kathy has helped me believe that we can be glad when we suffer because it makes us ready for what really matters and what will last forever.

Share your thoughts about why suffering is a more effective teacher than life's joyful moments.

....

....

....

....

What "knowledge of Christ Jesus my Lord" (Philippians 3:8) have you
gained from the seasons of suffering in your life?

....

....

....

....

*Lord God, the truth that I can be glad for suffering is so
countercultural and often so hard for me, in my sinful self-
centeredness, to accept. But I mean it when I call you "Lord,"
and I choose to accept what you allow in my life. Thank you
that you use the hard times to get me ready for eternity.*

I . . . count all things loss for the excellence of the knowledge of
Christ Jesus my Lord, for whom I have suffered the loss of all
things, and count them as rubbish, that I may gain Christ and be
found in Him, not having my own righteousness, which is from the
law, but that which is through faith in Christ, the righteousness
which is from God by faith; that I may know Him and the power
of His resurrection, and the fellowship of His sufferings, being
conformed to His death, if, by any means, I may attain to the
resurrection from the dead.

—PHILIPPIANS 3:8–11

Today I will, with faith—however shaky—in your love for me and in your healing power, reach out and touch the hem of your garment.

SHE HAD BEEN BLEEDING FOR twelve years, and, despite all the money she had spent on medical bills, no doctor had been able to help her. An outcast in society, penniless, and desperate, she decided to try to touch the hem of the Healer's robe. *What if I am able to touch him—and nothing happens? I have to try. How could my life be any worse than it is now?* Pushing through the dense crowd, she reached out her bone-weary arm and touched Jesus' robe. Suddenly something happened! It was as if someone had pulled open the drapes, and dazzling, healing light poured into the darkest part of her soul (see Mark 5:25–34).

Be encouraged by this woman's experience. First, she took a risk. She didn't succumb to that inner voice of shame that told her she shouldn't even show her face in public. Second, she reached out to Jesus himself. The body of Christ can indeed be vessels of healing love and hope, but we must never forget that Christ is the head. Third, this precious woman—the only person in all four Gospels whom Jesus addressed as "daughter"—told her story and allowed herself to be seen. She could have walked away when Jesus asked, "Who touched me?" Then she would have been physically healed but still sick at heart. So I encourage you to take the risk of going to Jesus for healing. He can release you from your shame and then use your story to encourage others.

What lies, if any, are keeping you from believing that God can and will do the same work in your life?

....

....

....

....

What will it look like to touch the hem of Jesus? Take that step.

....

....

....

....

Great Physician and Redeemer God, only in your power can I take the risk of asking, praying for, expecting healing—in your perfect way and your perfect time. Then, only in your power and by your grace, will I be able to tell my story to others. But what redemption that will be as you use my story to encourage others to go to you for healing and hope!

"If only I may touch His clothes, I shall be made well." Immediately the fountain of her blood was dried up, and she felt in her body that she was healed of the affliction.

—MARK 5:28–29

Today I will take my wounds to Calvary.

ONE EVENING A COUPLE YEARS ago I had the privilege of visiting a women's prison and spending the evening with some of the inmates—and what a rich time of worship we shared! Afterward, the assistant warden was kind enough to let me spend some one-on-one time with many of the women. One precious soul had written her story in a letter, and it was a heartbreaking tale of sexual and physical abuse much worse than anything I had ever heard described before. What impacted me was what she shared at the end: "God took me to a prison to set me free."

Some of the people who wounded her are gone from this earth; others refuse to acknowledge their guilt. But she is no longer a slave to any of them. She took her wounds to Calvary, and just as Christ forgave her for her sins, she forgave those who had sinned against her. And because of that she has been set free—healed from the most brutal of wounds. I will always remember her face. Although the lines around her eyes hinted at hard times, the quiet beauty and calm I saw were striking. Her face shone with the light of one whose wings were broken but who now soars again.

In what ways can one's inability to receive God's forgiveness or to forgive oneself be a prison?

....

....

....

....

....

....

Explain why our wounds can one day be seen as marks of God's grace.

....

....

....

....

....

> *Gracious and merciful God, I know the weight of sin and guilt—and I am so thankful that I know you as well, you who "will abundantly pardon." In these quiet moments, as I savor the forgiveness that you always have available to me, I ask that you would show me what I need to confess so that nothing blocks my relationship with you.*

Let the wicked forsake his way,
    And the unrighteous man his thoughts;
Let him return to the LORD,
    And He will have mercy on him;
And to our God,
    For He will abundantly pardon.

—ISAIAH 55:7

Today I will reaffirm my trust in the truth that you are my Deliverer.

I WILL DELIVER YOU! I didn't hear an audible voice, but in my spirit God's voice was unmistakable. I was startled by the clarity of the message. I often hear God speak through the Bible, my pastor, or my friends, but very rarely have I heard his voice be so commanding, clear, and deeply personal: *I will deliver you!* And I knew deep down exactly what situation God was assuring me that he would deliver me from. *But,* I thought, *how will God deliver me from this?* God answered that question quickly, clearly, and in his strong, loving voice: *I will deliver you!* At that point I knew the "how" had nothing to do with me. Not only that, but I realized that the "how" was ridiculous in light of the "who." All God was asking me to do was receive his promise and trust him. Nothing more.

From what do you need to be delivered? Perhaps you are weighed down by events in your past. Are you imprisoned by unforgiveness? Do recurring habits plague you and keep you from being the woman you want to be? Does shame—that internal tape telling you that you are hopelessly flawed and not worth loving—haunt you? Do you ever question the purpose of your life? Is fear a constant companion? Are you lonely? Are you feeling a degree of hopelessness? Whatever situation, emotion, or thought has its claws in you, I believe that God can deliver you!

Put down in black and white those things from which you need to be delivered.

....

....

....

....

....

....

Now list those characteristics of your Almighty heavenly Father which
make him more than able to deliver you.

....

....

....

....

....

> *Almighty God, you are my Rock, my Fortress, and my
> Deliverer! What comfort and hope I find in that truth! May
> I cooperate with you and your Holy Spirit for the work of
> deliverance you want to do in my mind, my heart, my life—
> and to you be the glory!*

The LORD is my rock and my fortress and my deliverer;
    My God, my strength, in whom I will trust;
    My shield and the horn of my salvation, my stronghold.
                                                    —PSALM 18:2

Today I will turn to you when emotions threaten to make me lose control.

EARLY IN OUR MARRIAGE, WHEN my words flew at my husband like hand-crafted missiles aimed right for his heart, I made an appointment to see a Christian counselor. His advice was simple: "Sheila, when you find yourself about to lose control, when you feel anger beginning to rise, then stop. Stop and ask the Holy Spirit to help you. Get down on your knees and throw yourself at the throne of mercy."

The counselor's advice sounded too simple, but he had given me the gift of truth. Going to the Lord was exactly what I needed to do, and the fruit of the presence of God's Spirit in my life was exactly what I needed to experience. Fruit, however, is produced; it doesn't just appear. It results from a growth process, and much happens beneath the surface of a tree's branches before any fruit is seen. Thankfully, the Holy Spirit is a Master Gardener who delights in working with scrawny, out-of-control bushes that grow slowly and yield only with great reluctance to his pruning. So now, when I want to cry out, "I can't help it!" I hear God's gentle Spirit reply, *I can.*

What emotion tends to make you lose control of yourself?

....

....

....

As you read Galatians 5:22–24 below, what does the Spirit offer you as a counterpoint to that emotion?

....

....

....

....

What can you do to be more mindful of the Spirit's transforming presence in you? Act on one of those ideas today.

....

....

....

....

Father God, I ask you to help me today to surrender my sinful nature to the Spirit's careful pruning so that I can be freer to love you and to do a better job of loving others.

The Spirit produces the fruit of love, joy, peace, patience, kindness, goodness, faithfulness, gentleness, self-control. . . . Those who belong to Christ Jesus have crucified their own sinful selves. They have given up their old selfish feelings and the evil things they wanted to do.

—GALATIANS 5:22–24 NCV

Today I will be still so that I can be aware of your presence with me.

I'VE INTRODUCED YOU TO DEBBIE. Now I want you to hear from her as she shares her thoughts in response to two hard questions. First, "Why are some people healed and others not?" Her thoughts: "Sometimes I wonder if God isn't giving me this time to reach out to others in similar situations. I feel as if there is something I still have to accomplish before I die. I pray I can. I want others to know they must accept Jesus into their lives so they can have eternal life. As I always say, only those prepared to die are really prepared to live. So I like people to say they are *living* with their disease, not *dying* from their disease."

The second question is "Why did it seem at first that I was all alone?" Debbie's comments: "My family has never left me, but most of my so-called friends have not stuck around. I guess most can't face the fact that I am going to die, but I wish they would realize that someday they are going to die, too, and that I'm still the same old me, maybe just a lot more fragile and thinner. When I first learned I do have a disease and I am going to die, I took a quick look at the Lord and a long look at my problems. I've learned to change this around, and now I take a quick look at my problems and a long look at the Lord."

What thoughts have you had about why God heals some people but not others?

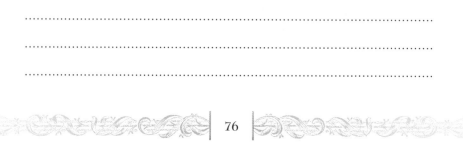

....

....

What hard question has come up in your life—and with what ideas do
you now respond?

....

....

....

....

Lord, life brings hard questions, and you don't always give me
answers that make sense to me at the time. But you do give
me yourself, and that, Lord, truly is more than enough for any
situation I encounter. Thank you for always being with me.

The LORD is my shepherd;
    I shall not want.
He makes me to lie down in green pastures;
    He leads me beside the still waters.
He restores my soul; . . .
Yea, though I walk through the valley of the shadow of death,
    I will fear no evil;
    For You are with me;
    Your rod and Your staff, they comfort me.

—PSALM 23:1–4

Today I will live with my eyes on you, Lord, both embracing and resting in what you have done on the cross.

IT HAS TAKEN ME MANY years to understand that God wants you and me to simply embrace what he has already done for us on the cross and rest in that forgiveness, reconciliation, and renewed relationship with him. I have also discovered—and maybe you have too—that when I am trying so hard to live a good life, my focus is on me. All I see is where I am flawed and failing. But when I take my eyes off myself and my performance, when I instead focus on the love of God and the companionship of Christ, I find not only amazing joy but real peace too. Jesus wants us to live in his victory. He has already overcome the enemy. He has already paid for our sin.

Yet the power of sin and the presence of evil in this world are both very real—but neither one is any match for the love of God. After all, God is in the redemption business, and Jesus has said that his grace will be enough for whatever we face. There is nothing you or I will face today, tomorrow, or ever that we will face alone. Jesus will be there with us, and he will provide everything we need to walk through it.

What can help you take your eyes off yourself and instead be more focused on the love of God and the companionship of Christ?

....

....

....

....

It's a promise: God's grace will be enough whatever circumstances we face. When has his grace clearly been instrumental in helping you deal with temptation, evil, loss, or pain?

....

....

....

....

....

All-powerful God, thank you that you make your power available to me when circumstances are tough, pain is overwhelming, thorns in the flesh are real, and life in this fallen world wears me down. I praise you for being my Redeemer and Friend!

Concerning this [thorn in the flesh] I pleaded with the Lord three times that it might depart from me. And He said to me, "My grace is sufficient for you, for My strength is made perfect in weakness." Therefore most gladly I will rather boast in my infirmities, that the power of Christ may rest upon me.

—2 Corinthians 12:8–9

Today help me to read your Word from a different perspective: I want to see your love on every page.

THE NEW TESTAMENT IS FULL of stories of people whose lives were radically transformed by the love of God—Mary Magdalene, Mary the mother of Jesus, the woman tormented by demons, a woman caught in adultery, one of the thieves crucified on Golgotha next to Jesus, to name a few. Seeing that pattern has prompted me to read the Bible with new eyes these days: no matter who the main players seem to be in a given scene, the story is about the love of God. It's not about us—about how good or bad we think we have been. It's all about our Father God and his beautiful Son, Jesus. And their love. Case in point.

Hear how Jesus himself once described his life's mission: "The Son of Man came to find and restore the lost" (Luke 19:10 MSG). Jesus didn't come to argue with religious leaders, heal those who were sick, or even paint a more accurate picture of his Father. Jesus came primarily to find and restore every lost human being, a work he ultimately did on the cross. And isn't it interesting that *the lost* can be translated as "broken beyond repair"? Have you ever felt broken to that degree, despairing, afraid you weren't going to make it? I love Luke 19:10 because it says that if we feel that way, we can take heart because that's why Jesus came. And that's love.

In what ways were you lost when Jesus initially found you?

....

....

....

....

....

....

In what ways, if any, are you lost now? What does the fact that Jesus loves you mean to you in your current circumstances?

....

....

....

....

....

....

Healing and Redeeming God, thank you for your love—love that seeks and finds the lost, love that brings healing and hope, love that redeems and guides, love that comforts, love that you have for me. And thank you for your Word where evidence of your love is found on every page. Great is your faithfulness, amazing is your grace, and humbling and wonderful is your love!

The Son of Man has come to seek
and to save that which was lost.

—JESUS IN LUKE 19:10

Today I will look for an opportunity to extend compassion, in the name of Jesus Christ, to someone who is hurting or in need.

COUNTLESS INDIVIDUALS AROUND THE WORLD—the sponsors as well as the sponsored children—have had their lives changed through the ministry of Compassion International. I know from experience, specifically, from a trip I made to a little school on the outskirts of Manila. One little girl caught my eye. When I asked about the small, quiet child, I learned that her name was Belinda and that she had no sponsor—and I said I would love to be her sponsor. After school, I went to meet Belinda's family in their shantytown home that was built over a swamp; the stench from the open sewers was unbearable.

Our Philippine interpreter explained to Belinda's mother who we were and why we were there. How would this poor woman, living in a one-room shack with ten children, react to our unannounced invasion? Nothing could have prepared me for the love that poured forth from her heart! She threw her arms around my neck and wept on my shoulder. I began weeping too, and we clung together, total strangers. As I looked into this mother's eyes, I was surprised by her hope and courage. She said, "The Lord's presence fills my home, and his glory is with us." We prayed together as best we could with our different languages, and I left with tears blurring my vision. I stopped to wipe the tears from my eyes, and when I looked down, there was Belinda's mother, on her knees in the mud, trying to wipe off my shoes.

When has an act of compassion extended to you been a dramatic illustration of Christ's very real love for you?

....

....

....

Where might you have an opportunity to extend compassion today? Walk through your day with open eyes and an expectant heart that is willing to act.

....

....

....

....

Hear me as I pray the prayer of Ignatius of Loyola: Teach us, good Lord, to serve Thee as Thou deservest; To give and not to count the cost; To fight and not to heed the wounds; To toil and not to seek for rest; To labor and not to ask for any reward Save that of knowing that we do Thy will.

I was hungry, and you gave me food. I was thirsty,
and you gave me something to drink. . . .
Anything you did for even the least
of my people here, you also did for me.
—JESUS IN MATTHEW 25:35, 40 NCV

Today I will extend kindness to someone who needs a comforting touch of compassion.

WOULD YOU WANT THE KIND of friends who came to Job's side after his tragic losses? I know I wouldn't! They were hardly compassion personified! Instead they showed shock and dismay. Oh, they were willing to spend time with him, but they didn't offer him compassion during those difficult hours. Their words were laced with accusation, argument, and judgment. True, they sat with him for seven days and seven nights in silence, but once Job broke that silence and began to cry out in his pain, his friends began a long, long harangue. Instead of comfort, they heaped on condemnation and the accusation we still hear today: "God is punishing you for your sins!"

Job must have felt terribly let down by his friends. Rather than showing him compassion, rather than extending pity, mercy, sympathy, kindness, or concern, they wanted to argue and prove him wrong—and they knew nothing of the agony he was suffering. In frustration, Job cried out with words that suggest how compassion should be expressed: "I also could speak as you do if you were in my place. I could make great speeches against you and shake my head at you. But, instead, I would encourage you, and my words would bring you relief" (Job 16:4–5 NCV). Job was saying that if he were our friend, he would cry with us, hug us, or hold us. He would show us God's love as we grieved.

Who has comforted you and therefore taught you how to come alongside those who are hurting? What can you learn from Job himself in Job 16:4–5?

....

....

....

....

....

Who in your path today might need comfort? Pray now and ask God to prepare you to extend kindness and compassion.

....

....

....

....

....

God of all compassion, my own acts of kindness and compassion need to start at home and in my neighborhood and among members of my church family. May I be sensitive to hurting people who are close to me—and may I also follow your lead as I seek to extend compassion to the poor, the downtrodden, the unlovely in my city and around the world.

If it were me, I would encourage you.
I would try to take away your grief.
—JOB IN JOB 16:5 NLT

Today I will not hide my faith; help me to show it not only with words but with actions too.

DID YOU KNOW THAT ARTIST Vincent Van Gogh was an evangelist early in his life? His mission organization sent him to a region in Belgium where the coal miners lived in desperate poverty. Van Gogh was provided with a nice house, but when he saw the shacks the miners were living in, he found it impossible to live in his much finer quarters. He probably told himself, *If I'm going to reach them, I'm going to live as one of them.* So he moved into a horrible shack, wore virtually nothing but a sack, and began to hold meetings. Eventually, people began to come to his meetings, and for six months he had an incredible impact in that area. Unfortunately, the head of his mission board visited. When he saw how Van Gogh was living—as one of the poor and downtrodden—the man was so disgusted with Van Gogh that he fired him.

Van Gogh had to leave the people he was trying to help, but they never forgot his sermons, which included statements like "For those who believe in Jesus Christ, there is no sorrow that is not mixed with hope." Van Gogh also said, "It's an old belief and a good one that we are strangers on earth, yet we are not alone, for our Father is with us."*

What was your reaction to the first paragraph's biography of Vincent Van Gogh? What thoughts came to mind? What emotions did you experience?

....

....

....

....

You may have been surprised to learn that Vincent Van Gogh—yes, the
artist who cut off his ear—was an evangelist. Who in your life might
be surprised to learn that you are a follower of Christ? Why would that
person be surprised—and what are you learning about yourself as you
consider this possibility?

....

....

....

....

> *God of grace, I never knew that Vincent Van Gogh once*
> *served you as an evangelist. I pray that people in my home, my*
> *neighborhood, my church, my workplace, my hobbies, and my*
> *recreational pursuits know that I am trying to serve you. Show*
> *me specifically, Lord, where I can be a brighter light and a*
> *more effective witness for you.*

Sanctify the Lord God in your hearts,
and always be ready to give a defense to everyone who asks you a
reason for the hope that is in you.
—1 PETER 3:15

---

* Irving Stone, *Lust for Life* (New York: Doubleday, 1934).

Today I will find hope in you for the people I know who are lost.

WHEN HAVE YOU FELT LOST? Are you heavy hearted even now because someone you love is lost? Here is some good news for you: Jesus came to seek and save those who were lost, however they got lost (Luke 19:10).

- Some of us, for instance, don't intend to be lost; we don't mean to become separated from the body of Christ. We just wander off for a while, seeing what is in another's field, and suddenly it's dark and we can't find our way home. Jesus says, "I will go looking for this one when it starts to get dark, and I will carry him home."
- Others of us feel that our lives are dropped and lost. One woman, who had a divorce dropped on her out of the blue, told me that it felt as if someone had cut the string that held her life together, and she fell and rolled under the sofa—and no one even noticed she was gone. The good news is that you are never lost to God. He knows exactly where you are. When no one else sees or cares, he does, and he will find you and help you begin a new life.
- And then there are those of us who choose to walk away from God. Know that he is always waiting for us to come home. When we finally come back—and not necessarily because we miss him—our heavenly Father will welcome us with quite a bash. Our Father waits and welcomes back into his arms each one who walks away.

Jesus' parables about the lost sheep, the lost coin, and the lost (or prodigal) son speak powerfully of the depth of the Father's love for us no matter whether we or someone we know intended to walk away, were dropped and lost, or turned from God in bold rebellion. And that truth about his unfailing love is very good news!

You may already have a prayer list, but if not, start one now and list people you know who are lost and spend some time praying for each one.

....

....

....

Also spend some time talking to your heavenly Father about the times you have been lost or felt broken beyond repair . . . and he came to you with love.

....

....

Faithful, loving God, thank you that I am never so lost or so broken that your love can't bring renewal to my heart and my life. And thank you that this truth applies to those people—my family members, friends, neighbors—who are lost. Nothing is impossible for you, my all-loving Father!

Rejoice with me,
for I have found my sheep which was lost!
—THE SHEPHERD IN LUKE 15:6

Today I will choose to believe that you are faithful and that you use hard times to make me more like Jesus.

IF GOD LOVES ME, WHY *did my child die? . . . If God hears my prayers, why am I still single? . . . If God is in control, why is life so hard? . . .* You may be able to add your own hard question to this list. Whatever that question is, the answer remains the same—and it's a choice of faith—"Life is tough, but God is faithful."

And God's faithfulness doesn't guarantee an easy journey through life. In fact, he promises exactly the opposite: he promises that in this life we will have trials and tribulations, hardship and pain (John 16:33). Yet he who is sovereign and wise and loving and good also promises that the tough times aren't wasted. According to Romans 8:28–29—and I'm on a personal campaign to always refer to those two verses together!—even the most difficult, most painful times of life are used by God for our good, and that good is to be more like Christ . . . more trusting of our heavenly Father, walking more closely with him, being more free from sin's grip, able to love others more wholeheartedly, finding ourselves more sensitive to the Spirit's guidance and instruction, being more joyful whatever life's circumstances. And I'm sure you can add to the list. Life *is* tough, but God *is* faithful!

When have you asked God hard questions? What were the circumstances that prompted the questions, and what were the questions?

....

....

....

....

When have you experienced the sweet presence of God in the midst of
bitter pain and suffering? Would you trade in that bittersweet season of
your life? Why or why not?

....

....

....

....

> *Lord God, I don't know why you allow things—tragic and*
> *painful things—to happen in my life and in this world. But I*
> *also know that a god I could totally understand and explain*
> *wouldn't be the almighty sovereign God of the universe. So*
> *I'm choosing to trust you and believe in your faithfulness.*
> *I believe; help my unbelief.*

We know that God causes everything to work together for the good
of those who love God and are called according to his purpose for
them. For God knew his people in advance, and he chose them to
become like his Son.

—ROMANS 8:28–29 NLT

Today I will be totally honest with you when I come to you in prayer.

I HAVE AN AMAZING ANNOUNCEMENT to make: it is impossible to stink at prayer! Don't laugh! If you had asked me ten or twenty years ago to evaluate my spiritual life, I would have told you that I stink at prayer, and I had pretty much resigned myself to that fact. But change does happen, and now I firmly believe that, although we may feel like we stink at prayer at times, God gladly receives our words. Any prayer is a gift to him, for it means we are talking to him. I believe that when we recognize God is always with us—and he is—every breath can be a prayer. Prayer is not just a few sentences we say to God while on our knees. Prayer is the living out of our ongoing, every-moment commitment to God.

And listen to this. God hears all our prayers, the good and the bad. He is big enough to handle our honest questions, our doubts, and even our anger. God receives our thankful prayers and the not-so-thankful ones, the eloquent ones and the less-than perfect ones. He accepts our joyful and self-confident prayers as well as our anguished questioning when we experience trauma or loss. I've gone to God when I was afraid, angry, and therefore very honest. It felt good to relate to God in that authentic way—and I could never go back to my old, edited, controlled prayers. Real relationship demands intimate dialogue. Know that God accepts all our prayers because when we pray, we acknowledge our belief that God is in control.

Which statement about prayer do you find most striking and/or most encouraging? Explain why.

....

....

....

....

What interferes with your having that ongoing dialogue with God you
would like to have?

....

....

....

....

*Father God, I was thinking. . . . Maybe becoming like little
children means becoming more authentic, unedited, natural,
spontaneous, constant in our prayers. We all know kids who
are delightful chatterboxes who say what they're thinking
and feeling, who haven't necessarily learned to think before
they speak, and who expect all that they say to be regarded as
important. Free me, I ask, to talk to you as little children talk
to their trusted parents.*

I tell you the truth, unless you change and become like little
children, you will never enter the kingdom of heaven.

—JESUS IN MATTHEW 18:3 NIV

Today I will look to you to reveal my sin to me so I can humbly rejoice in your forgiving love.

IT WAS 5:30 THE EVENING before Thanksgiving. I needed to get out of the office and into a grocery store—and that's when my secretary told me that a young woman named Jennifer was in real trouble and needed to talk to me. I was already behind schedule, but I knew I'd feel guilty and not enjoy Thanksgiving if I didn't call Jennifer. So I called, and the conversation went from bad to worse until Jennifer said, "I didn't call wanting you to get angry with me. Why are you angry with me? I thought you would pray for me." I had blown it. Big-time blown it. We did pray together, we hung up after I reassured Jennifer that she could call me again, and I wept. . . .

Sometimes the most loving thing God can do is to hold up a mirror before our faces and let us gaze at the stark reality of what we're really like. I hadn't been honest with my secretary: "I'm tired. Could you get one of our phone counselors involved?" I hadn't been honest with the Lord: "I don't want to make this call, but someone needs my help so I need your help. Please give me your love and wisdom for this hurting person." And I hadn't stopped to pray. I thought I could handle this call in a few minutes and be on my way. Well, I learned a good lesson that day: one of the keys to living the Christian life is to have healthy humility and to be ever aware of the dangers of subtle pride.

When was the last time you didn't stop to pray and regretted taking action without consulting God?

....

....

....

....

....

What is key to having a healthy, godly humility?

....

....

....

....

....

....

*Thank you, Lord, that you love me too much to let me stay
stuck in my sin. Thank you that you show me my sin so I
can confess, be forgiven, and, in your power, change my ways.
Please help me maintain a healthy humility and teach me to
not take a step without you.*

**Pride leads to destruction;
a proud attitude brings ruin.**

—PROVERBS 16:18 NCV

Today I will ask you to help me recognize the lack of forgiveness in my heart that may be fueling impatience and rage.

HARDLY A CRIMINAL OFFENSE, BUT apparently an unforgivable sin. At least that was the conclusion of a woman I saw in the grocery store when—horror of horrors!—a gentleman was paying for eleven items in the "ten items or fewer" line! Oh, she had counted his purchases aloud for everyone to hear, and, genuinely embarrassed, the man offered to put one item back. When the checker graciously told him that wasn't necessary, the Offended One became more furious. She used a bucket of verbal water to put out a single matchstick, and I'm sure she fumed all night as she schemed how to wreak revenge on the next eleven-item customer!

But let's see what may have been fueling that woman's rage. Perhaps at some point in her life, this woman was seriously wronged by someone, yet she never received the healing of forgiveness; she was never able to let her pain go for fear it would diminish the significance of the wrongs done against her. When negativity begins to take over, transgressions big and small can begin to pile up until something like eleven items in the ten-item grocery line puts you over the edge. Consider how many times you have found yourself grousing at someone, knowing full well the real reason for your discontent is another matter entirely. Why not let go of your frustration, trusting that God who sees all will take care of things in his own time?

What recent or relatively recent occasion of your overreacting suggests you have some frustration to let go of and some forgiveness to extend?

....

....

....

....

Spend a few moments thanking God for his forgiveness of you, forgiveness that cost his Son death on the cross.

....

....

....

....

Just and wise God, you know better than I the lack of forgiveness I harbor even though I self-righteously look down at people who overreact to a given situation because of the lack of forgiveness that they, too, nurture. Enable me to identify that lack in my life and to forgive.

Then the scribes and Pharisees brought to Him a woman caught in adultery. . . . He raised Himself up and said to them, "He who is without sin among you, let him throw a stone at her first."

—JOHN 8:3, 7

Today I will keep my eyes on the cross, a picture of Jesus' love for me.

IT CHANGED MY PERCEPTION OF the Cross. I'm talking about the question "Do you know how much Jesus loves you?" and the answer "This much," an answer illustrated with arms outstretched just as our Savior's were when he was hanging on the cross. His nail-scarred hands, stretched voluntarily across the rough wood and held there by iron pegs that pierced his flesh and made him bleed, speak volumes of Jesus' amazing love . . . for you.

Life's bumpy road, however, can have any one of us doubting God's love and fearing what the next day or week or month will hold. I don't know what kind of past you are dealing with or what fears have resulted from your journey through life. But I do know this: God is love, and his love is far bigger than any past circumstances, current fear, or worry about the future that can try to distract you and keep you from focusing on him. "Let us," as the author of Hebrews says, "fix our eyes on Jesus, the author and perfecter of our faith, who for the joy set before him endured the cross, scorning its shame, and sat down at the right hand of the throne of God" (12:2 NIV).

Who in your life has loved you with a love that makes Jesus' love for you more real? Thank God for that person and, if possible, thank that person as well.

....

....

....

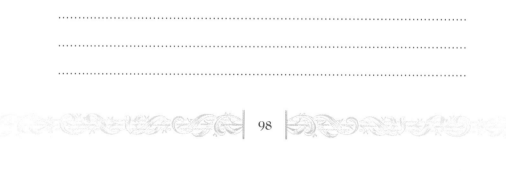

....

....

....

....

What, if anything, keeps you from wholeheartedly believing that God loves you? Whatever it might be—a past experience, a lie you don't recognize as such, the hesitation to believe that God truly and completely forgives you, or something else—write it down here. Bring it out into the light so God can help you deal with it.

....

....

....

....

....

....

Lord, as I am better able to embrace your amazing love for me, help me to love others too.

God is love. . . .
There is no fear in love;
but perfect love casts out fear.

—1 JOHN 4:16, 18

Today I will appreciate your touches of compassion and grace in my own life.

HERS IS AN AMAZING STORY! While those five words could be said about many women in the Bible—perhaps every woman—I want to spend some time today revisiting Mary Magdalene's story. We don't know a lot about her life before she met Jesus. We do know that, at that point, she was possessed by seven demons, each of which Jesus cast out of her. But before that powerful touch of grace, imagine what it was like to be taken over by the prince of darkness and his twisted cohorts. What relentless agony of soul and spirit! Mary must have felt there was no way out of the nightmare that was her life. Thankfully, Jesus rescued Mary from the kingdom of darkness and put her feet on a path right beside his.

Blessed by Jesus' gracious act of deliverance, the healed and whole Mary traveled with him and his disciples. She saw miracles performed and lives transformed—and she saw Jesus handed over to the soldiers and nailed to a cross on Calvary. Mary watched as Joseph of Arimathea wrapped Jesus' body in clean linens, laid him inside a tomb, and rolled a stone in front of the entrance. Then, before dawn, Mary was back at the garden tomb with spices to anoint the broken body of Jesus—but the stone had been rolled away! The body was missing! Panicked, Mary ran to find Peter and John, and together the three hurried to the tomb. The weeping Mary stayed there after the two returned to the other disciples. That was when she heard her name: "Mary." The resurrected Jesus chose to show himself first to Mary. He appeared before the very person who had been tormented by the legions of hell. She was the first to see that Satan, her enemy, was defeated and that Jesus her Lord held the keys to life and death.

What do you now better appreciate about Mary Magdalene's amazing story?

....

....

....

When has Jesus' victory over Satan and death been especially meaningful to you?

....

....

....

....

Compassionate and gracious God, I love that your resurrected Son first appeared to Mary Magdalene, that she was the first to see that he had defeated her longtime enemy and tormentor! How perfect is that! How perfect are you! I love you!

[Mary Magdalene] turned around and saw Jesus standing there, and did not know that it was Jesus. Jesus said to her, "Woman, why are you weeping? Whom are you seeking?" She, supposing Him to be the gardener, said to Him, "Sir, if You have carried Him away, tell me where You have laid Him, and I will take Him away." Jesus said to her, "Mary!" She turned and said to Him, "Rabboni!" (which is to say, Teacher).

—JOHN 20:14–16

Today I will ask you to help me start learning how to live in total freedom from the past.

SHE CAREFULLY OPENED THE BOX and peeled back layer upon layer of soft, pink tissue paper. Nestled inside was the most beautiful dress she had ever seen. It was exquisite—white with satin ribbons that tied in a bow at the waist. When she put it on, it fit as if it were tailor made. Not given to spontaneity or dancing, she nevertheless found herself twirling round and round—until she caught sight of herself in the mirror, light, free, and almost childlike. She stopped immediately, took off the dress, put it back in the box, and slid the box under her bed. She took her old gray dress off the chair, pulled it over her head, and straightened her hair in the mirror. "There," she said. "That's how it should be."

But is that how it should be? One of the greatest challenges to living as the women God sees us to be is our very own memory bank. We remember all the poor choices we have made and wonder how our life could have been different. We look back at times when we were not strong or didn't know ourselves well, and we chastise ourselves for being . . . human. We blame ourselves for things that were not our fault. We play old tapes in which we talk to ourselves in a way we would never dream of talking to anyone else. It's hard to shake things we've believed for many years.

What keeps you from wearing the exquisite dress of freedom from the past?

....

....

....

....

....

What do you think God wants you to do with that exquisite white dress?
Look at the cross and consider what that dress of freedom cost him!

....

....

....

....

....

> *Redeemer God, thank you for sending Jesus to free me from
> the pain of the past and to give me a future and a hope. By
> your Spirit, help me to bring all the old negative habits to you
> and leave them there. Deliver me from the pain of the past and
> redeem my scars . . . for the sake of your kingdom.*

There is therefore now no condemnation to those
who are in Christ Jesus, who do not walk according to the flesh,
but according to the Spirit.

—ROMANS 8:1

Today I will not judge others.

HAVE YOU NOTICED THAT WE are really good at rank ordering sin? It is so tempting to categorize sin, but God's grace has nothing to do with our scales of human justice. From our perspective, it's easy to pick out the good guys and the bad guys, but God says there is no such thing as a good guy. We are all sinners standing in need of God's grace and forgiveness. But if you're like me, you've thought, *Well, sure, I understand that we're all sinners in a broad sense, Lord, but there are some of us who mess up a lot less than others. You can't tell me that doesn't count for something.* Well, actually, it doesn't count for anything.

Again, it is so tempting to categorize sin, to see others as less deserving of God's grace than we are. The clarion call of a grace-filled life is that we are required to lay down our internal scales of justice, not only as we see ourselves but also as we see and judge others. In terms of our salvation and God's love for us, our list of what we view as our good behavior counts for nothing.

Why does our enemy love that we rank order sin?

....

....

....

....

....

....

....

....

....

What would help you get rid of your internal scale of justice once and
for all?

....

....

....

....

....

....

....

....

*Gracious Father, it's not fair; it's grace. And, Lord, as I open myself
to receive your grace, may I focus my eyes on you. Your grace is
all about you. It's not about me; it's not about how I compare to
others. Your grace is all about you. . . .*

From heaven the LORD looks down to see
    if anyone is wise enough to search for him.
But all of them are corrupt;
    no one does right.

—PSALM 14:2–3 CEV

Today I will, by your grace, be sensitive to judgments I make about people and remind myself that I don't know their story.

I MET HER AT A women's conference. My son, Christian, was about to turn twelve; her son was already out of high school. Hoping to pick up a few tips, I encouraged her to keep talking when she said, "I wish I had known what I know now when my son was twelve." And her boy's story—a tragic tale of drug and alcohol addiction—came pouring out. She had adopted her son when he was just a baby and had no idea he had a strong genetic pre-disposition to addiction. He gave his life to Christ as a young boy and has prayed over and over to be delivered, but the battle is fierce. He has been in and out of treatment programs wrestling with the demons that torment him. And this precious mother's greatest heartache has been watching how others in their church treated her son. Her words were powerful and convicting.

"If he had a brain tumor or cancer, they would be over with casseroles and flowers. But there are no flowers for my boy. People don't understand he is sick. They just think he is weak or a bum," she said with tears in her eyes. With tears in my own eyes, I had to admit to myself that I had never thought of drug addiction or alcoholism that way. The reality is that those whose brains are wired toward addiction go through tremendous pain if they try to break free. Everything within their bodies and brains craves the next hit the way a man lost in the desert craves water. And, in addition, those who battle addiction often feel the pain and isolation of the church's judgment.

When have you heard the background story of a person you had come to an inaccurate conclusion about? What lesson can be learned from that humbling experience?

....

....

....

....

Who in your life currently might you have come to an inaccurate conclusion about? Ask God to show you—and know that he may bring to mind people whom you feel self-righteously superior to.

....

....

....

....

Merciful God, where I have been guilty of judging others, please show me and help me make my heart and, if necessary, my relationships right. In any area where I have a heart of stone even now, please soften my heart and fill it with your love and grace.

Judge not, that you be not judged. . . . Why do you look at the speck in your brother's eye, but do not consider the plank in your own eye?
—JESUS IN MATTHEW 7:1, 3

Today I will, by the power of your Spirit, more fully embrace your amazing love for me—and respond with Christlike love for those around me.

THE MORE IN LOVE WE are with the Father and with our Savior, the more we become like Jesus himself. And that's not unique to the relationship between our Creator God and us, his creation. Maybe you've noticed that couples who have been married for a long time say that they know each other well enough to be able to complete the other person's sentences. Imagine having that same relationship with God—to communicate with him so intimately and often that we know his thoughts well and can complete his sentences. Imagine the benefits of such a relationship; imagine the strength and peace that would come with that kind of loving and that sense of being loved.

God longs to share his heart with us. He is not looking for perfect little robots programmed to follow his directions, but for people who will receive his love and love him and others in response. I think it's very difficult for us to embrace the love of God because we have never been loved that way before. That's because all human love—even the best we have experienced—is conditional and is impacted by our behavior or changing circumstances. But God's love is not. God wants people who will share his heart and work with him for things that have eternal worth.

In what ways would your life—your thoughts, words, and actions—be different if you walked around every day with a deep awareness of the truth that you are overwhelmingly loved?

....

....

....

What steps can you take toward living in the truth that God's love for you is immeasurable, unconditional, and unshakable?

....

....

....

God of love, may the truth that you love me not just be a fact I hold in my head, but a truth that lives in my heart and guides me 24/7. You love me . . . I sit in awe of that truth, feeling thankful and blessed, humbled and joyful. Thank you for your love—and teach me, in response, to love you and others well.

Love suffers long and is kind; love does not envy; love does not parade itself, is not puffed up; does not behave rudely, does not seek its own, is not provoked, thinks no evil; does not rejoice in iniquity, but rejoices in the truth; bears all things, believes all things, hopes all things, endures all things. Love never fails.

—1 CORINTHIANS 13:4–8

Today I will be looking for evidence of your presence and your work in my life.

HAVE YOU EVER FOUND YOURSELF at the end of a day thinking, "I had no idea when I woke up today that by tonight my life would have changed so much"? Perhaps you just discovered that you are going to be a mom, or perhaps you heard the doctor say, "Your cancer is back." One day can definitely change the landscape of a human life.

Think of Moses standing before the burning bush, or Mary learning she was pregnant by the Holy Spirit. What about Noah being given the assignment to build an ark bigger than a football field, or Simon Peter being called from his career as a fisherman to be an itinerant preacher? Then there was the shepherd David chosen to be king of Israel and the Christian-killing Saul chosen to be the amazing preacher/evangelist/church planter/theologian Paul. These are dramatic examples of God's life-changing power, a power we encounter in quieter moments as well . . . such as when he comes alongside to calm our worries, to remind us of his faithfulness, to shine his guiding light into the darkness of our confusion, to touch our hearts with hope when circumstances seem hopeless, to whisper to us of his love. Even a gentle touch from the Father can change the landscape of our life.

What day in your life, if any, came to mind as you read the first paragraph of today's devotional? Describe in detail what happened and what made that day so significant.

. . . .

. . . .

. . . .

. . . .

. . . .

Sometimes instead of changing our circumstances, God changes our hearts. When have you experienced that kind of his work in your life? Thank him for it.

. . . .

. . . .

. . . .

. . . .

. . . .

Lord, I don't need drama; I just need you. Help me to rest in your promise that your plans for me are plans for good—and help me to follow your lead and cooperate with your Spirit as those plans unfold.

"For I know the plans I have for you," declares the LORD, "plans to prosper you and not to harm you, plans to give you hope and a future."
—JEREMIAH 29:11 NIV

Today I will make an effort to stay satiated with your grace that I may more readily and easily extend your grace to others.

MY SON IS NOT A big breakfast eater. On a summer morning he will often run out to shoot hoops with nothing more than the aftertaste of toothpaste in his system. Then he'll come dragging in and say, "Mom, I'm starving!" And maybe you can relate. Do you ever find yourself spiritually starving halfway through your day? Remember that fresh grace is available moment by moment, from the second you open your eyes until you crawl back under the covers at night.

And maybe you've noticed this truth: when we keep ourselves satiated with God's grace, we find it much easier to extend grace to others. If we are on starvation rations, we will have little grace to spare. In other words, we'll find it tough to extend to others what we have not allowed ourselves to be blessed by. So let's nail down some basics right now: God loves you. . . . He knows all that is true about you, and he loves you. . . . Even when you can't forgive yourself, he forgives you. . . . There is nothing you can do to make him love you more. . . . There is nothing you can do to make him love you less. . . . This is the grace of God.

What can you do—or what do you do—to keep tapping into the fresh springs of God's grace, available to you 24/7?

....

....

....

....

....

Think about the people God has placed or allowed in your life. To whom do you most struggle to extend grace? Why do you think that is—and what will you do about that struggle?

....

....

....

....

God of grace, thank you for the grace you extend to me 24/7 . . . for the grace that made me recognize your grace in the first place . . . for the grace that holds me close to you and will never let me go . . . for the grace that keeps you loving me. Thank you—and please use me to extend your grace to others.

You know the grace of our Lord Jesus Christ, that though He was rich, yet for your sakes He became poor, that you through His poverty might become rich.

—2 CORINTHIANS 8:9

Today I will choose to take the risk of forgiving someone who may hurt me again.

WHAT IF I FORGIVE SOMEONE *and that person hurts me again?* Perhaps you've asked that very question, and it's a good one. Forgiveness does mean we could get hurt again in exactly the same way by the very same person we just chose to forgive. In that sense, forgiveness is something we do without knowing the outcome—we don't know the impact, if any, our forgiveness will have on our relationship with that person—and that not knowing is hard. We would have an easier time forgiving if we knew that, upon hearing our words of grace, the person would then apologize, be appropriately remorseful, and never hurt us again. But when we forgive someone who turns right around and does the same hurtful thing again—and that happens—not only are we wounded afresh, but we also feel foolish.

Life is hard, people are unpredictable, and the benefits of our forgiving someone who has hurt us are uncertain. But we have access to a Father who can comfort us when the bullies and deceivers come our way. He can also comfort us when we obey his command to forgive and get hurt again by the person we forgave. God never said life would be easy; he did say that he will always be there for us.

In what relationship, if any, are you reluctant to extend forgiveness because you are afraid of getting hurt again?

....

....

....

....

....

....

What do you think the Lord wants you to do in this situation—and why?

....

....

....

....

Just and holy God, you know that we human beings don't always treat one another kindly, respectfully, or justly, and that truth makes it tough for me to want to forgive people who have hurt me. May my fear of being hurt be overshadowed by the truth that you'll be with me even if I am hurt again. Help me, Lord, to do what is right even though it's hard.

Bear with each other and forgive whatever grievances you may have against one another. Forgive as the Lord forgave you.

—COLOSSIANS 3:13 NIV

Today I will count the cost of forgiving and the cost of not forgiving.

"I DON'T BELIEVE THAT PERSON is really sorry" and "Saying 'I forgive you' won't take away the pain"—these are two reasons why people (even Christians and maybe you) are reluctant to forgive someone who has hurt them. That first excuse is validated by the fact that our society—even our Christian community—has downgraded forgiveness. Forgiveness is not a Band-Aid for a wound; that wound has to be recognized for what it is, grieved over, and owned before forgiveness can be real, freeing, and lasting. To minimize someone's pain with a "Hey, I'm sorry, friend" and perhaps even a quick prayer—without truly acknowledging any wrongdoing and its very real consequences—is an offense in itself. You may never receive a genuine apology from the offender, but what do you gain by allowing your wound to fester?

As for the second concern above, I believe we can only really forgive when we acknowledge both the truth that we are wounded and the depth of that wound. It is tempting to slough pain away and deny that we have been hurt. It can be embarrassing to be wounded: we feel weak or out of control, so we ignore it. We need to accept that we live in a world where pain is sometimes just part of the package. Once we humbly admit that we are wounded and allow ourselves to feel the pain, we can bring it to Christ for healing; only then can we begin the process of forgiveness. And, yes, it is a process.

Why is whether or not a person is genuinely sorry for hurting you irrelevant to the issue of forgiveness?

....

....

....

....

....

Why is it significant that forgiveness is a process?

....

....

....

....

....

Lord God, as I think about forgiveness, I am thankful for the truth that when you call your people to do something, you empower us to do that very thing. Lord, please work in my heart that I might be able to obediently forgive and to be patient with the process.

Then Peter came to Him and said,
"Lord, how often shall my brother sin against me, and I forgive him? Up to seven times?" Jesus said to him, "I do not say to you, up to seven times, but up to seventy times seven."

—MATTHEW 18:21–22

Today I will open myself to the work you want to do in my heart.

MY GRANDFATHER—MY MOM'S DAD—WAS A hardworking man with a simple faith. At mealtimes, his standard grace was "For what we are about to receive, may the Lord make us truly thankful." On one particular occasion, when they were having guests for lunch after church, my grandmother asked him to embellish his usual blessing a bit. Maybe he forgot her request because he started off with his usual "For what we are about to receive, may the Lord make us truly thankful." After a noticeable pause he added, "And make me a good boy, amen!"

My grandfather's simple—if unexpected!—prayer raises an important question: does the actual act of prayer, of throwing ourselves on the mercy and grace of God, change us? Was there a kernel of truth in my granddad's precious prayer—that just by being in God's presence, we become "better" boys and girls? I think so. In fact, I strongly believe that prayer impacts the one praying. And, truth be told, I thirst for a prayer life that is so intense and moment-by-moment that I cannot help but be changed. How about you?

When have you been aware of the positive impact praying has had on the person who is praying, on either yourself or someone you know?

....

....

....

....

....

....

Danish theologian Søren Kierkegaard has observed, "Prayer does not change God, but it changes him who prays." Does this statement make sense in light of the God of the Bible you know?

....

....

....

....

....

Creator and Redeemer God, I've always known that there is more going on than I'm aware of when your people pray to you. Whenever I come before you, may I pray expectantly, looking forward to hearing your voice, knowing your presence, seeing you answer prayers in your good and perfect way, and transforming me! Thank you for caring enough about me to want to grow me and make me more like Jesus—and thank you that prayer is a tool you use.

We, who with unveiled faces all reflect the Lord's glory, are being transformed into his likeness with ever-increasing glory, which comes from the Lord, who is the Spirit.

—2 CORINTHIANS 3:18 NIV

Today I will take a step toward freedom and away from the brokenness in my past.

HIS FATHER WAS A VIOLENT alcoholic who beat his family members every day. His mother's paranoia made her no source of comfort. Furthermore, she tended to set the two brothers up in competition with each other. This young man realized that nothing he accomplished would ever be enough to please his parents. Even when he later gave his life to Christ, he still dealt with fear that was rooted in the pain of his childhood—but now he didn't deal with it alone. Every time he sensed the beast of fear and shame approaching, he could invite the love of God into that dark place.

What kind of brokenness have you experienced? Whatever it is—however irreparable the damage seems—you can do what my friend does and what I do: invite God's light into that darkness. Ask God to flood every part of your wounded soul with his love and to shine his light into every dark corner. You can fall on your knees and take any crippling thoughts about your past or haunting fears for your future to God's throne of grace. Although he does not guarantee us pain-free passage through this world, he does promise the companionship of Christ and a peace that passes understanding.

Light brings healing to wounds, comfort to fears, and guidance to confusion. In what specific ways has God—who is light—been any or all of those things to you? Give a few examples.

....

....

....

....

....

What kind of darkness currently in your life do you want to bring
before the Lord? Prayerfully do so now and be ready to receive God's
love and peace.

....

....

....

....

....

> *Lord God, as a resident of a very dark world, I praise you
> who are light for guiding me through the darkness . . . for
> healing me of the consequences of dark choices made by others
> and myself . . . and for freeing me from fear that comes in the
> dark. I invite you to flood every space in my heart and every
> question in my spirit with your love and peace.*

God is light and in Him is no darkness at all.

—1 JOHN 1:5

Today I will let go of a past sin that continues to torment me.

YOUR HEAD MAY KNOW THE wondrous truth that, by Jesus' death on the cross, God has removed your sin from you as far as the east is from the west and that he chooses to remember it no more. If you—as I did at one time—find it hard to let the impact of that good news sink right into the depth of your heart and soul, try something that helped me. When I have felt burdened by a past failure or persistent flaw, I've written it down on a piece of paper, taken that issue before the Lord, and then burned the piece of paper. Let me give you an example.

I noticed that, in order to feel accepted, I had a tendency to say that I'd seen a movie or heard a CD when I hadn't. So one day I wrote this on a piece of paper: "Father, sometimes I say things that aren't true because I want people to like me. I know this is wrong, lying is a sin, and I ask you to forgive me." Then I lit the piece of paper and threw it into the fireplace. As it burned, I thanked my Father for his grace that covers my sin. As I watched the burning paper turn to ashes, I knew that—by God's grace—I would never again have to let that confessed and forgiven sin torment me. I pray that this exercise works for you.

Why do we sometimes fail to confess certain sins?

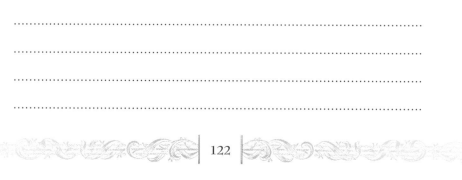

....

....

....

What secret sin are you carrying, or what confessed and forgiven sin
still haunts you? Take it before the Lord right now—don't wait a second
longer—as I did with my sin. Let the Holy Spirit set you free.

....

....

....

....

....

....

....

*Holy Lord, your forgiveness is a gift precious beyond words,
an act gracious beyond description, and, for various reasons,
sometimes hard for me to accept. Please help the wonderful truth
that you have forgiven my sins penetrate my heart and set me free.*

As far as the east is from the west,
    So far has He removed our transgressions from us.

—PSALM 103:12

Today I will practice clinging to the cross of your Son, my Savior.

HOW CAN I MAKE GOD love me more? What do I need to do to be worthy of God's love? Why does God answer some people's prayers, but not other people's? Why do I feel so far away from God? For years I asked myself questions like these. That's because for years I missed the point of the gospel the way each of us sometimes misses the point of a joke. I had totally missed the message of God's faithfulness and love. I didn't "get" the finished work of Christ on the cross. When life was tough, I still wondered what I had done wrong. Even though I read the Bible over and over, I still worked hard to make God love me. After all, so much human love and acceptance is based on performance, or on being thin enough, pretty enough, smart enough, or "whatever" enough.

But after almost forty years, I truly "got" it; I finally and truly understood the message of the gospel. I realized the truth that none of us will be able to stand unless we daily throw ourselves into the saving arms of God. First of all, I recognized that our life on this earth is not about us. And then I realized that we can't live in our own power the life of faith we want to live. We have no strength apart from God. Basically, what finally became clear to me was the message of a hymn I remember from my childhood: "Nothing in my hands I bring; simply to Thy cross I cling."

What are you clinging to today instead of the cross? The Holy Spirit will show you if you're not sure. Just ask him.

....

....

....

....

....

What does—or would—clinging to the cross of Christ look like in your life? Be specific. Again, the Holy Spirit loves to be asked that kind of question.

....

....

....

....

....

It's hard for me to accept the truth that there's nothing I can do to earn my salvation, to gain greater acceptance from you, or to make you love me more. In fact, in my own power, I can't live a life that pleases and glorifies you. So, with nothing in my hands, I come to you wanting to learn to cling more tightly to your cross.

By grace you have been saved through faith,
and that not of yourselves;
it is the gift of God, not of works,
lest anyone should boast.

—EPHESIANS 2:8–9

Today I will look to you, Lord, instead of to the past and what-if scenarios.

HAVE YOU NOTICED THAT THE what-if game can fuel some crazy imaginings? *What if I hadn't . . . ? Or what if I had . . . ?* But perhaps more often than not, what-ifs fuel bitterness, anger, and grief. *What if I hadn't done what I knew was sinful? What if I had obeyed God instead?* And, sadly, these what-ifs too often keep us focused on self, beating ourselves up for blowing it, rather than looking to God, the One who redeems our missteps, intentional and otherwise.

Are you living in the shadowy land of what-ifs? It happens, but you don't have to stay there. And you—and I—shouldn't. Whenever I find myself overwhelmed with thoughts of my past—or fears about my future—I have to catch myself, get down on my knees, and take those thoughts, regrets, and fears to the throne of grace. We followers of Jesus are not guaranteed safe, comfortable, or pain-free passage through this world, but we are promised the companionship of Christ and a peace that passes human understanding. Take him up on that offer today! Receive his peace and enjoy his company!

For the final—and perhaps the first time—confess to your heavenly Father the what-if scenarios from your life that fuel guilt, shame, discouragement, or fear. Leave them at his feet.

....

....

....

....

....

....

When have you sensed Jesus' companionship during life's hard times?
What specifically has he done to make his presence with you known?
Thank him.

....

....

....

....

....

....

{ *Lord God, please guard my heart against the what-ifs that can
bring me down. And teach me to live with confidence in the truth
that you, my King and my Redeemer, have overcome the world
and are at work redeeming my missteps.* }

In the world you will have tribulation;
but be of good cheer, I have overcome the world.

—JOHN 16:33

Today I will consider what I am doing with my life: am I pursuing an earthly reward or a heavenly one?

THE VIET CONG LANDMINE BLEW his six-foot, two-hundred-seventy-pound body of rock-hard muscle in half. Bob Wieland came home two feet, ten and a half inches tall and weighing eighty-seven pounds. After Bob was lying for five days in a field as his blood drained out on Vietnamese soil, medics finally found him. He remembers coming to and thinking, *Well, Lord, they tried to finish me off here, but I'm still alive. So what do you want me to do? What purpose do you have for my life?* Choosing not to lose hope, Bob set to work on a new goal, that of establishing a world record as a weightlifter. The day finally came when Bob gripped three hundred and seventy pounds and, with one supreme effort, lifted it above his head to establish a new world record. But soon the title was taken away: he was disqualified because someone had discovered a rule on the books that said you had to wear shoes while lifting a weight in competition.

How angry does that true story make you? It still makes me furious, that we human beings can be so petty! But I digress. Learn—as I have—from Bob's reaction. When I talked with Bob about this unjust incident, he smiled and said simply, "What could I do? I looked into the judge's face, shook his hand, and told him, 'I understand. That's all right.'" Bob's response showed me that he grasps a truth that no book other than God's Word can teach: *No earthly crown is ultimately worth anything.* Bob decided to remember that God is faithful—and I imagine that on that day they took away his weightlifting medal, a jewel of far greater, of infinite value, was placed in his heavenly crown.

Why do you think God wanted you to hear Bob Wieland's story?

....

....

....

....

What earthly crown are you pursuing with perhaps too much energy, time, or passion invested? Keep in mind it ultimately won't last.

....

....

....

....

> *Holy God, forgive me when I am discontented and self-pitying. Forgive me for pursuing earthly crowns. Forgive me when I am petty and critical of others. . . . Clearly, the story of your servant Bob Wieland has touched my heart. Thank you for your grace in his life—and thank you for your grace in mine.*

I have fought the good fight, I have finished the race, I have kept the faith. Finally, there is laid up for me the crown of righteousness, which the Lord, the righteous Judge, will give to me on that Day, and not to me only but also to all who have loved His appearing.

—2 TIMOTHY 4:7–9

Today I will speak to someone you send my way about the difference Jesus has made in my life.

LET ME SHARE ONE MORE scene from Bob Wieland's remarkable, sold-out-for-Jesus life. . . . God gave Bob the new dream of doing something for the homeless in America. What that involved was a "walk" across America to raise money for the homeless—and Bob didn't let his missing legs stop him. Wearing special gloves that were built like shoes, Bob took off, propelling his weight with nothing but his arms and hands on a coast-to-coast journey that took three and a half years. Everywhere he went—and in all kinds of weather!—Bob asked God to give him an opportunity to speak to people about the difference that Jesus has made in his life. One day he had traveled mile after mile without seeing a car, so he asked the Lord, "Before I go to bed tonight, could you give me two people? Perhaps a car could stop, and I could talk to two people about you."

It was almost dusk when a car pulled up beside him. An older couple got out and talked with Bob for a long time about many things. Eventually Bob said, "Can you see any reason why you shouldn't give your lives to Jesus right now?" The two of them said they could not, and they joined Bob there on the side of the road, on their knees, and prayed to receive the Lord as their Savior. And that older couple, whom Bob had led to the Lord on that dusty road, were his own mother and father.

Think about your own salvation story. In what way(s) was God's sovereign choreography evident?

....

....

....

....

Think right now about the differences Jesus has made in your life so that
you are ready when God brings you someone who needs to hear about
Jesus and about the hope you have in him.

....

....

....

....

*Lord, Paul's words below could easily be mine: I want to be
able to speak as I ought to speak, to clearly explain the mystery
of Christ, when you open the door for me to share the gospel
with someone who is lost. May I be faithful—and may I rely
completely on you—when you give me that opportunity.*

Continue earnestly in prayer, being vigilant in it with
thanksgiving; meanwhile praying also for us, that God would open
to us a door for the word, to speak the mystery of Christ, for which I
am also in chains, that I may make it manifest, as I ought to speak.

—COLOSSIANS 4:2–4

Today I will choose to stay on the altar as a living sacrifice to you.

SUFFERING IS SELDOM AN ITEM on our list of requests to the Lord. But when it crosses our path—and it does and it will—we are reminded that life is not a walk through the park. In tough times, we can see that life is actually a worship service and that each of us is invited and redeemed to be a living sacrifice to God. As living sacrifices, we could crawl off the altar when the heat and pain get too intense, but that is not the way to glorify God with our lives.

Now, we Christians say that we are willing to learn lessons from God, but our attitude really says—especially when the flames are roaring around us— "Hurry up, Lord, and get on with it. I need to get this over with. If you have to teach me something that will help me be a better Christian, okay. But if you could do it before lunchtime, I'd be very grateful, because I really do have a full schedule." Understanding why the flames are blazing and learning a life- or heart-changing lesson in the first five seconds of the fire—this is not always God's will for us either. Instead, when we are able to keep on walking with him and living for him—and we can only do this by his grace—our lives become messages of hope to the world and to the church.

Why do we struggle to stay on the altar as a living sacrifice to God? Is it an issue of trust, control, and/or something else? What do you think?

....

....

....

....

....

....

Whose life has been a message of hope to you? Who has, by God's grace, chosen to stay on the altar during inexplicably difficult and painful times? Talk about what that person has taught you about being a living sacrifice to the Lord.

....

....

....

....

....

> *Lord God, teach me to keep my life on the altar—for my good and your glory—so that you can use me as a message of hope to the people who know that flames are burning strong in my life.*

When you pass through the waters, I will be with you;
    And through the rivers, they shall not overflow you.
    When you walk through the fire, you shall not be burned,
    Nor shall the flame scorch you.
For I am the LORD your God,
    The Holy One of Israel, your Savior.

—ISAIAH 43:2–3

Today I will remember that you see me and that you enable me to endure.

YOU MAY KNOW HAGAR. SHE was the maid of Abraham's wife Sarah, and her story is found in Genesis 16–21. One remarkable scene from her life occurs when, after being forced to sleep with Abraham, becoming pregnant, and being made miserable by Sarah (who, trying to help God fulfill his promise to Abraham, originally had the culturally appropriate idea that Hagar sleep with Abraham!), Hagar runs away. As she struggles alone in the wilderness, an angel of God appears to her and tells her to go back to Sarah. The angel promises Hagar that her son would be the first in a great nation of people, and Hagar called God *El Roi*, which means "the God who sees."

This simple story is quite remarkable in at least two ways. First, for the slave girl Hagar to be able to call Jehovah God "the God who sees *me*" is striking. This is the first time in Scripture that God was called by such a personal name. Also, Hagar did obey the angel: she returned to Abraham and Sarah's home—not an easy assignment—where she gave birth to Ishmael—which certainly wouldn't quench Sarah's jealousy. Don't you find it interesting that Hagar did as the angel said? What we learn is, when we know God is with us, we can endure most things. It's only when we feel as if we are alone that we lose hope.

When have you tried to help God—as Sarah did—and have things not turn out exactly the way you had hoped? What prompted you to offer God assistance? What did you learn from this experience?

....

....

....

....

....

When we know God is with us, we can endure most things. For what current situation in your life is this truth a real encouragement? What evidence of God's presence do you see in that set of circumstances? Be encouraged!

....

....

....

....

Forgiving Lord, thank you for your grace at those times when, like Sarah, I do not patiently wait on your timing, I try to help you, and I feel overwhelmed by jealousy. Help me to be more like Hagar, aware that you see me and that you are with me, enabling me to do whatever you call me to do.

The angel also said, "You are now pregnant and will give birth to a son. You are to name him Ishmael (which means 'God hears'), for the LORD has heard your cry of distress." . . . Thereafter, Hagar used another name to refer to the LORD, who had spoken to her. She said, "You are the God who sees me."

—GENESIS 16:11, 13 NLT

Today I will remember that my only hope is in you and that you are with me always.

HOPE IS REALIZING THAT YOUR destiny is interwoven with God's sovereign power and will for your life, and Psalm 139 strengthens my hope like few other passages in the Bible. The lines of that psalm beautifully describe how the Lord is always with us—every moment of every day and every night.

> Where can I go from Your Spirit?
> Or where can I flee from Your presence?
> If I ascend into heaven, You are there;
> If I make my bed in hell, behold, You are there.
> If I take the wings of the morning,
> And dwell in the uttermost parts of the sea,
> Even there Your hand shall lead me,
> And Your right hand shall hold me. (vv. 7–10)

Job desperately needed to know God's presence. If only God would make himself plainly known, Job would have something to count on, something to keep his hope alive. And, toward the end of the story, God finally appeared to Job in all his sovereign power and glory. And, after hearing from the Lord a thunderous barrage of unanswerable questions, Job admitted that he had talked about things that he did not understand and that he had spoken of things too wonderful for him to know. Job never received an answer to his first question— "Why?" But Job did gain the new understanding that his only hope was in God.

What encouragement for today do you find in Psalm 139:7–10?

....

....

....

What "why?" in your life are you willing to let go of as an act of hope, an act done in light of the fact that your destiny is interwoven with God's sovereign power and will for your life?

....

....

....

Sovereign Lord, I bow before you, awed that you would want to be with me every moment of my life—and thankful that you are. I also bow before you, humbly aware that I have demanded answers to my question "Why?" when, like Job, I would be wise to choose to trust your will for my life and to rest in the truth that my only hope is in you.

> I know that you can do all things
>   and that no plan of yours can be ruined. . . .
>   I talked of things too wonderful for me to know. . . .
> My ears had heard of you before,
>   but now my eyes have seen you.

—Job in Job 42:2–3, 5 ncv

Today I will be sensitive to your nudging me to move out of my comfortable Christianity.

HARRY WAS A WHITE MAN living on the streets who was embraced by a small Hispanic church, loved with Jesus' love, and nurtured in his faith. Listen to something Harry told me when he was thinking back on that amazing and life-saving demonstration of God's love and grace: "You know, Sheila, so often we're prepared to take our hands off and say, 'Well, Jesus is the answer.' But you know, Sheila, *we* are the answer. You and I. Jesus has left us a job to do."

And when we do that job—when we reach out with Christ-like compassion to hurting, struggling, lonely, lost souls—we will experience the joy that comes with doing God's will. Doing that job, however, will involve leaving the comfortable confines of our own lives, of our self-indulgent and self-satisfied Christianity. We will no longer simply sit at home struggling with our own failures and temptations. In fact, one of the first steps of reaching out to others in the name of Jesus is taking your eyes off yourself. As we look around instead of inward, we will easily find places to share a cup of cold water in our own community, sometimes right on our own block. Go—and be blessed as you are a blessing.

Take a long, hard look at your life. What evidence do you see, if any, that your Christianity has become self-indulgent and too comfortable?

138

....

....

....

....

Who in your church and/or neighborhood needs your compassion? List the names below and beside each name note what you can do for each person. Act on one today.

....

....

....

....

Holy Spirit, thank you for showing me the ways I have let my faith become self-indulgent and too comfortable. Continue to work in my heart and my life so that I will not only notice opportunities to be compassionate but will also act selflessly for God's glory and another person's good.

Faith by itself isn't enough.
Unless it produces good deeds, it is dead and useless.
Now someone may argue, "Some people have faith; others have good
deeds." But I say, "How can you show me your faith if you don't have
good deeds? I will show you my faith by my good deeds."
—JAMES 2:17–18 NLT

Today I will look for opportunities to serve—and I will serve whatever the task.

"Footwashing for Beginners." I think that should be a required course at every church and definitely a course required for every new believer. Why? Because the moment we enter the kingdom and family of God, we need his help in understanding and then living out a basic and very counter-cultural principle: we are called to serve—and the Suffering Servant himself calls us to that. Jesus uses a figure of speech right out of dry, dusty Palestine where open sandals were standard footwear. Animals—whose masters were seldom concerned about where those critters left their waste—shared the same unpaved roads. Everyone's feet needed to be washed before reclining at a table and sharing a meal!

None of the disciples at the Last Supper, however, was willing to get down on his knees, pitcher and towel in hand, and wash the feet of his fellow disciples. Jesus himself seized this teachable moment. The meal was barely underway when the King of kings and Lord of lords, knowing the spiritual, emotional, and physical turmoil that would soon tear his soul apart, stood up, removed his outer clothing, wrapped a towel around his waist, and began washing his disciples' feet (John 13:4–5). Peter objected, realizing that one of the Twelve—every single one of the Twelve—should have done the service. But Jesus had known their hearts—and ours: full of pride, hungry for status, well aware of tasks that are beneath our dignity. Jesus knew what it meant to be a servant. I wish we all could more readily follow his footsteps.

When has serving in a menial and behind-the-scenes capacity been a blessing to you? Comment on why that might have been the case.

....

....

....

....

What ongoing opportunity for service that you've been aware of might be God calling you to step into? Make it a matter of prayer.

....

....

....

....

Lord, forgive my arrogance and pride. They too often function as blinders (I don't see opportunities to serve) and as heart-hardeners (I decide that a certain task—if I even notice it—is beneath me). Please give me your heart, the heart of a servant, and may I serve you by serving others with genuine joy.

Whoever wants to become great among you
must serve the rest of you like a servant.
—MATTHEW 20:26 NCV

Today I will remind myself of the good reasons you allow me to experience tough times.

THE ISRAELITES WERE ENSLAVED BY the Egyptians. . . . After 430 years of backbreaking captivity—and a set of remarkable plagues—Pharoah finally let them go. . . . Changing his mind, though, Pharoah sent his army to attack Israel. . . . God delivered his frightened people as the terrifying chariots bore down on them. . . . Then, because of their choices, the nation of Israel wandered in the desert for forty years, wondering if they had made the wrong decision when they left Egypt. . . .

Why did God allow his chosen people to experience such tough times? To learn the heart of their God. To understand that they were loved and treasured. To come to appreciate and accept the need to put their complete faith in God. And to see how capable they really were when they did put their faith in him. And these are the same reasons God allows us, his children, to experience tough times today. Bottom line, I believe that one of the most powerful fruits of testing is to begin to finally grasp that although we are weak, in Christ's strength, we are strong. Each time we are tested and each time we stand strong in his grace, we grow in our knowledge of him and in our confidence that he is our strength (Philippians 4:13).

What kind of testing has the Lord allowed you to go through?

....

....

....

....

....

....

....

Review the reasons why God allows us to undergo such tests. Which of
these fruits have you experienced to one degree or another?

....

....

....

....

....

....

*Almighty, sovereign, loving God, I praise you for today's
reminder that there is nothing random about what has
happened, what is happening, and what will happen in my life.
As I undergo these tests that—by your grace—make me more
like Christ, may I know your strength in my weakness.*

I can do all things through Christ who strengthens me.

—PHILIPPIANS 4:13

Today I will model my responses to Satan's temptations after Jesus' perfect examples: "God is my provider. . . . I will not take the easy way out. . . . I will not seek the spectacular; I will seek God's face."

SATAN TEMPTED JESUS THREE TIMES, and the third time he encouraged Jesus to show off his Sonship, to opt for style over substance, to choose spectacle over obedience. "Wouldn't it be quite the display of divinity," Satan suggested to Jesus, "to throw yourself down from the top of the temple and have God's angels catch you before you hit the ground?" Knowing that God wasn't at his beck and call to respond to unwise and risky behavior, Jesus refused to go along with the enemy's idea. Jesus stood strong against the Deceiver.

Satan can and will test us in many ways just as he tested the Son of God. We can give in. We can desire what we don't have. We can want glory without suffering. Or we can look to Jesus, who modeled for us perfect responses for encounters with Satan: "God is my provider. . . . I will not take the easy way out. . . . I will not seek the spectacular; I will seek God's face." Whatever situation you are facing right now, know that Jesus left his footprints in the desert sand for you to follow. Also, keep in mind that whatever Satan tempts us with is never what we are really longing for. What he offers may appear to meet a need at the moment, but he will just take us deeper into the wilderness. Following Christ's steps keeps us close to the heart of God.

In what ways does our culture tempt us to opt for style over substance?

....
....
....
....

Explain the difference between testing God and taking a step of faith.

....
....
....
....
....

"God is my provider. . . . I will not take the easy way out. . . . I will not seek the spectacular; I will seek God's face." May these statements keep me strong just as they kept you strong in the wilderness, Lord Jesus!

Draw near to God and He will draw near to you.
—JAMES 4:8

Today I will take my emptiness before you, anticipating what your transforming power will do.

THE NEWS BEGAN WITH A whisper. *Messiah has come!* So people began to follow Jesus, waiting to see what he would do. Would he quietly gather an army and then establish God's kingdom? What the Messiah did as his first sign of who he was, was very different from what people expected: he turned water into wine at a wedding in Cana. Of all the miracles of Christ, this seems the least life-changing. Oh, it was fabulous for the family as everyone left the reception talking about how lovely the bride looked and how amazing that wine was! But is that the extent of what Jesus actually did at the wedding? No, there is much more.

Here is what I believe the gift of this water-to-wine miracle is to us today. The servants brought their empty jars to Jesus, and he told them to fill them with water. Similarly, we are to take to Jesus whatever we have. After the servants returned, Jesus touched the ordinary water with his power, transforming it into something wonderful. Not only that, but the volume produced—one hundred to one hundred and fifty gallons—was far more wine than the people at the reception could possibly need. This miracle, therefore, is a sign to you and to me that Jesus can take our ordinary lives and transform them with his grace into something far greater than we can ask or imagine.

What causes you to feel empty or ordinary? If you're feeling that way today, what has contributed to those feelings?

....

....

....

....

What encouragement do you find in the miracle Jesus did at the wedding in Cana? What message does the Lord have for you today?

....

....

....

....

....

> *Lord, thank you for including the story of this miracle in your Word. I often feel like ordinary water, so it's encouraging to see what your transforming power and immeasurable grace can do! Today I take to you my ordinary life. May you continue your work of turning it into something wonderful.*

Nearby stood six stone water jars . . . each holding from twenty to thirty gallons. Jesus said to the servants, "Fill the jars with water"; so they filled them to the brim. Then he told them, "Now draw some out and take it to the master of the banquet." They did so.

—JOHN 2:6–9

Today I will—with your help—not play the comparison game and instead focus on taking joy in your plan for my life.

WHEN I WAS PREGNANT WITH Christian, I had a very honest conversation with a friend of mine. We were the same age, and she longed to be married and be a mom. I married Barry when I was thirty-eight and was gifted with a child at forty. She told me that it was hard to realize that we both came before God about the same time with the same requests, and God gave me a husband and a child while she received neither. I ached for my friend. Her questions made total sense to me. . . .

Will you and I choose to recognize that God knew what he was doing—that we was acting in his perfect wisdom—when he lovingly put things in your life and lovingly put different things in mine? Only when we can accept his hand working differently in your life than he does in mine, answering each prayer in his own time and according to his own and higher understanding, can we truly be at peace with God. Believing the lie that God is not listening to us dampens our relationship with him. But taking joy in living out his plan for us—that's freeing!

The comparison game isn't fair or healthy, for no one really knows the burdens another carries. When have you been amazed to learn the painful or difficult story of a person you thought you'd trade places with in a heartbeat?

....

....

....

....

....

....

What aspects of God's plan for your life can you truly take joy in today?

....

....

....

....

....

....

God of joy and hope, God of goodness and freedom, I ask that you would teach me to embrace your plan for my life—but not just intellectually. May I take joy not only in the unique plan you have for me but also in the truth that you are with me each step of the way as that plan unfolds.

I have learned in whatever state I am, to be content.

—PHILIPPIANS 4:11

Today I will marvel at the fact that you chose me to be one of your precious daughters.

I WILL NEVER FORGET THE night I was baptized in my home church in Ayr, Scotland. I was sixteen years old, and several of us were being baptized by our pastor, Reverend Edwin Gunn. When it was time for the baptisms, we made our way to the stairs at the side of the baptismal tank. One by one, each of us climbed the stairs and went down into the water. Before he baptized me, Pastor Gunn took my hand and said, "Sheila, I asked the Lord for a verse for you, and he gave me this: 'You did not choose me but I chose you. And I appointed you to go and bear fruit, fruit that will last, so that the Father will give you whatever you ask him in my name'" (John 15:16 NRSV). With that, he lowered me into the water. When I came up, it was all I could do not to shout and dance. I felt as if I had been kissed by God!

God chose me. I couldn't get that wonderful truth out of my heart. No one had ever chosen me before, and now I was chosen by God! But what exactly did that mean? From this point on, would everything in my life fit neatly into place? Would all my imperfections be perfected? I'm a little embarrassed by this admission now, but I wondered if my skin might have cleared up and if I might have left a few unwanted pounds in the water! Surely if God chose me, he might want to make life a little easier for me. I have, however, come to understand that what Jesus wanted—and still wants—is to live his life in and through me, not to fulfill a few teenage dreams that might have changed my outward appearance but done nothing for my heart.

What does it mean that God has chosen you? Be specific about the impact that truth has on your heart and on your life.

....

....

....

And what does it mean that Jesus wants to live his life in and through you? Be as specific as possible—and if you're not sure, make this a topic for prayer and conversation with other believers.

....

....

> Loving God, your own Son was despised and rejected by men (Isaiah 53:3), and I know all too well those feelings of being hated and rejected, of not belonging and not fitting in. Yet you, in the mystery of your grace, have chosen me to love, to be part of your kingdom, to belong to your family. Thank you that I am chosen by God!

What is man that You are mindful of him,
Or the son of man that You take care of him?
You have made him a little lower than the angels;
You have crowned him with glory and honor,
And set him over the works of Your hands.
You have put all things in subjection under his feet.

—HEBREWS 2:6–8

Today I will be thankful that I don't know the future and choose contentment in the present.

IT WAS A CHRISTMASTIME FAMILY reunion in Scotland. As if the joy of Jesus' birth weren't enough, I was introducing my two-year-old son Christian to my Scottish family, and I was meeting my three-year-old nephew Dominic for the first time. Yet God had an unexpected gift for me as I stood on the Scottish soil where I was raised. Feeling as if I had come full circle, I was overwhelmed by the grace and mercy God had poured into my life. Standing there, I remembered the tears I had shed as a child, not understanding why I had to be the only girl in my class with no dad. I remembered the awkward teenage years, hating my body as it started to develop and feeling embarrassed and unlovable because of my greasy hair and bad skin. I remembered the years of running at full speed for God, trying to impress him with my manic devotion. I remembered the first few days in that psychiatric ward, feeling hopeless and sad and lost. . . .

At that moment, though, as I stood at the edge of the cold winter sea, I was wrapped in God's blanket of love. Running just ahead of me, my precious bundle of grace and joy was chasing seagulls. Beside me was Barry, my wonderful, loving, funny, kind husband. Tucked into the pockets of my soul were two years of sharing my life with women and seeing with my own eyes the way that God shines through the broken places of our lives, bringing hope and life. I knew that this moment wouldn't be so sweet if had known the future at any time along the way. The agony of earlier moments of despair made that moment even more miraculous and joyful. Yes, God is faithful.

When, if ever, have you realized how glad you were that you hadn't known the future? Explain.

....
....
....
....

When, if ever, have God's blessings been sweeter because of the hard times you had known earlier?

....
....
....
....
....

Eternal and wonderful God, I praise you that you are the same yesterday, today, and forever; that you will always be gracious, loving, merciful, kind, just, compassionate, righteous; and that you will always be providing for me, protecting me, and blessing me with your presence. I praise you, Lord, and am blessed to call you Father.

Jesus Christ is the same yesterday, today, and forever.
—HEBREWS 13:8

Today I will keep praying about the matter that you seem to be saying "no" to . . . because "Be with me" is more important than "Why?"

I'M SURE IT'S A MYSTERY you've bumped up against more often than you would have liked. I'm talking about the great mystery and challenge of living with unanswered prayer when we know that God is both all-loving and all-powerful. After all, if God were just *loving*, then when our prayers went unanswered, we'd make peace with it by telling ourselves that if he were powerful, he would have intervened. Or if God were *powerful* but not loving, we would not be surprised that he didn't respond to our pain. But God loves us with a passion that exceeds our understanding, and he is powerful enough to intervene in any situation, at any moment, and change our circumstances. Sometimes he does do that, but more often he does not.

Jesus Christ himself lived through his Father saying "no." Remember Gethsemane? I reject with everything that is in me the argument that Jesus, fully God and fully man, knew the great joy and victory ahead and so didn't mind knowing he would soon die an excruciatingly painful death on the cross. Jesus was fully man, and he suffered as a man would (although without sinning). He knew that his Father would not deliver him in this situation. But Jesus knew that even when God was telling him no, God was still with him. You and I learn that, too, when we keep praying despite God's no. And as we keep praying, we move beyond "Why?" to "Be with me, Lord." Confronting God with our why becomes being with God in our need.

When have you wrestled with the issue that your all-loving and all-powerful God nevertheless chose to not answer your prayers?

....

....

....

....

....

Spend some time right now talking with your Father. He already knows your heartache and the reason for it. Let him come near to you now.

....

....

....

....

> *God of compassion, may I know your presence with me in very real ways when I don't know why you let my prayer go unanswered. . . .*

"Father, if it is Your will, take this cup away from Me; nevertheless not My will, but Yours, be done." Then an angel appeared to Him from heaven, strengthening Him.

—JESUS IN LUKE 22:42–43

Today I will live with mystery rather than ranting against you and your ways that are beyond my understanding.

THE EIGHT-YEAR-OLD BOY WROTE, "You say God can do all sorts of things. Please ask God if he'll make my mommy love my daddy." . . . The fifteen-year-old girl living on the rough streets of Chicago asked, "Can God be interested in someone like me?" . . . Another young girl called to say that she was being sexually abused by her father and her uncle and that she couldn't turn to anyone for help because no one would believe her. . . . This list can go on and on, this list of situations where we want to see God's hand move and make a difference, make everything all right. Yet heaven often seems silent, mute, uncaring. Why?

I don't know the answer to that question. I don't believe anyone fully does. But God has brought some very brave and godly people into my life who have helped me understand that there are no easy answers and to accept living with mystery when there is no visible reason to do so.

What events in your life or in the life of someone you know has made you question why heaven seems silent, mute, and uncaring?

....

....

....

....

....

What do you want to say the next time someone asks you why God doesn't seem to care about them or isn't responding to their prayers?

....

....

....

....

....

....

Lord God, our human ways are not your ways. Your thoughts are not our human thoughts. Your ways and thoughts are higher. Perhaps that gap—a gap of mystery between you and us humans—exists at least in part to keep us looking up to you.

"For My thoughts are not your thoughts,
    Nor are your ways My ways," says the LORD.
"For as the heavens are higher than the earth,
    So are My ways higher than your ways,
    And My thoughts than your thoughts."

—ISAIAH 55:8–9

Today I will keep my inner eyes on you, trusting you and accepting life's trials even though I don't like them.

WHEN SHE WAS EIGHTEEN, MAROLYN Ford's eyesight began to fail. Soon all that remained was a little peripheral vision, and the Mayo Clinic diagnosed her condition as two ruined retinas caused by macular degeneration. Doctors were sorry, but nothing could be done. She would be blind for life. Despite this bleak prognosis, Marolyn kept living life. She went to college, got married, and had a daughter—and all along the way she kept her inner eyes on Jesus. "I didn't have to like my blindness, but I needed to accept it. I knew the Lord had a reason for it, and my prayer was 'Dear God, if I have to be blind, let it not be in vain.'"

One night after getting home from church, where Marolyn was the choir director, she and her husband got down on their knees to pray once again. This time when her husband cried out to God for healing, suddenly, inexplicably, miraculously, Marolyn could see perfectly. It was a total and wonderful miracle—of which her eye doctor said, after spending a great deal of time peering into her eyes, "There is no medical explanation for why you can see with those two eyes. When I look into them, all I see is black scar tissue where it should be smooth and pink." By God's grace, those eyes continue to see more than ten years later.

For what situation does Marolyn's experience encourage you to pray for God's divine intervention and miraculous touch? Keep praying!

....

....

....

....

....

For what can you praise the Lord even if he hasn't yet brought healing?
What great things has the Almighty done for you?

....

....

....

....

....

*Lord, I love it when your work baffles science! You are
amazing! And, Lord, help me to keep praising you even when
you choose to answer prayers in ways that you deem best, but
in ways I don't understand.*

My soul magnifies the Lord,
And my spirit has rejoiced in God my Savior. . . .
For He who is mighty has done great things for me,
And holy is His name.

—LUKE 1:46–47, 49

Today I will bow before your sovereignty and thank you for making me who I am.

WHEN YOU FIND YOURSELF WITH a few quiet moments, do you ever wish that you were someone else? I imagine that, at some point, every single woman on the planet has reviewed the portfolio of her life and wished for something different. Does someone else's marriage seem happier, her kids better behaved, and her relationship with God blessed by continuously answered prayer? Or perhaps you are confined to a wheelchair, slowed down by a degenerative disease, or caring for a special-needs child. Are such physical challenges divine mistakes? Are your particular circumstances some cosmic accident?

First of all, I know that in God's original plan, life was never meant to be this way. The brokenness we suffer from was not God's choice but, through Eve, it is ours. Now the whole planet limps along, yet I believe in the midst of the world's weeping you are you for a reason. You are not an accident; you are a woman with an eternal destiny. It takes some of us a long time to understand that. Often that understanding comes only as we choose to let go of what we think should have been and instead bow our hearts to the sovereignty of God. Will you do that?

Do you believe that you are you for a reason? Do you believe God made you just as you are and that you are not a mistake? If so, why? If not, why do you struggle with that?

....

....

....

....

....

Is there an aspect or event in your life that you think is an accident? If so, ask God to help you see it as he sees it.

....

....

....

....

....

Sovereign God, I ask you now in the powerful name of Jesus to help me see my life as you see it—and to help me see myself more the way you see me. Deliver me from the lies of the enemy, lies I have heard so long and repeated so often that I mistake them for your voice. Help me, I pray, to love my life as you love it.

All the days ordained for me
were written in your book
before one of them came to be.

—PSALM 139:16 NIV

Today I will turn to *you* and to no one and nothing else for love, acceptance, purpose, and a sense of belonging and significance.

HUMAN BEINGS HAVE COME A long way . . . in the wrong direction . . . since Eden. There in the garden, Adam and Eve were fully known and fully loved by their Creator. They could walk and talk with God, eagerly listening for and easily hearing his voice. The Lord was with them, as ever-present as the wind, and they basked and blossomed in his presence. With their rebellion, Adam and Eve lost their innocence; they lost their intimate relationship with God and with each other. God's love for human beings did not fall, though. God has not changed at all. Our ability to receive his love has been damaged, but not one ounce of God's love for us has diminished.

Everything that you and I are looking for in this life—acceptance, belonging, love, significance, purpose—can be found in the arms of our heavenly Father. The challenge is finding our way back to him. Key to that is setting our fixed gaze on God our Father. With our eyes on him and our heart open to receiving his love, we will grow in our confidence that—whatever pain and heartache happen in life—God himself will always be with us, Jesus will walk beside us, and the Holy Spirit will bring comfort and strength. It is a glorious thing to be loved like that. So may you hold on tightly to God and only to him. You don't have to take one more step or cry one more tear alone. You don't have to face one more decision or one more day of sickness alone. You are loved, and you are never alone.

In what moments of your life have you found human love disappointing?

....

....

What difference does the truth that you are loved and never alone make in your life—or what difference would it make if you fully embraced this truth?

....

....

God of love, I confess that I am guilty of trying to find in people the kind of love that can be found only in you. Forgive me, Lord, and reprogram me. Point my eyes to the cross of Christ. Sensitize my heart to your constant love. And, by your Holy Spirit, give me the grace to live in your loving presence every minute of every day.

But the eyes of the LORD are on those who fear him,
    on those whose hope is in his unfailing love, . . .
We wait in hope for the LORD;
    he is our help and our shield.
In him our hearts rejoice,
    for we trust in his holy name.
May your unfailing love rest upon us, O LORD,
    even as we put our hope in you.

—PSALM 33:18, 20–22 NIV

Today I will let myself begin to believe a little bit more that you adore me.

GOD ADORES YOU JUST AS you are. That's worth reading again, isn't it? God adores you just as you are. He doesn't look at you and think, *Did you mean to get your hair cut like that? Who told you that you looked good in yellow? Couldn't you have done better?* Many of us will ask ourselves questions like these because a negative, critical voice has, for various reasons, taken up residency in many of our heads and hearts. So, again, know that God adores you just as you are, and I believe he wants to set you free to live in his love right now. It may take some spring-cleaning of those negative messages, though, so let's get to work.

Take a piece of paper and, with the Holy Spirit's help, write down all the negative things you can remember for as far back as they go and wherever they came from—your parents, your husband, someone in your family, a teacher, or a bully at school or work. Write down everything you can think of that made you feel bad about yourself. Then, when you pray the following prayer, give every single item on that list to Jesus and let his blood wash away everything you have written down. Those messages don't belong to you. God adores you. He is not disappointed in you. You are his beloved daughter, fearfully and wonderfully made, and he wants you to kick up your feet and dance.

Who in your life has given you a taste of God's unconditional love? Describe that person's love for you and explain why it has been a gift to you.

....

....

You've listed things you have believed about yourself that are not true. What have you believed about God that isn't true? Ask the Holy Spirit to show you your false ideas and, from the Word, God's truth.

....

....

....

God my Shepherd, you know my heart—the wounds it has sustained, the confusion about who you are and who I am that it harbors, the lack of forgiveness that provides an illusion of strength, and the desire I have to truly know, trust, and rest in your love for me. As I tear up this list of hurts—of words and experiences that have made me feel bad about myself—please help me open myself to your love and receive it. I would love to believe that you adore me!

Joyful are those who have the God of Israel as their helper,
    whose hope is in the LORD their God. . . .
He gives justice to the oppressed
    and food to the hungry.
The LORD frees the prisoners.
    The LORD opens the eyes of the blind.
The LORD lifts up those who are weighed down.
    The LORD loves the godly.

—PSALM 146:5, 7–8 NLT

Today I will sit at your feet.

I'M GUESSING YOU REMEMBER THE sisters, opposites in temperament but both devoted to Jesus. Martha was busy waiting on Jesus and his disciples when they came to dinner—and Mary sat at Jesus' feet. Now imagine stopping by for coffee the next morning and asking them, "What was the most important thing Jesus said last night?"; "Which of his statements have you carried with you into this new day?"; and "What do you understand now that you didn't understand yesterday morning?" Their answers would have been as different as their personalities.

Many good books and insightful articles have been written about the differences between these two women who were devoted to Jesus, and many of these writers offer ideas about how we can have Mary's heart in our hyperdrive busy world that calls us to be a Martha. But perhaps we need only the marketing slogan "Just do it!" rather than any textbook. So join me today in sitting at Jesus' feet and learning from him, worshiping him, and pouring out your life as an offering to him. Let's just do it!

Which sister—Mary or Martha—are you more like by nature? Support your answer with specific details.

....

....

Everyone is busy, and full schedules can make it hard to find time to be with Jesus. But what internal factors—if any—also keep you from slowing down and spending time with your Lord? Talk to him about it. Ask the Holy Spirit to do his transforming work in your heart and mind.

....

....

....

....

....

....

God, no matter how long my "to do" list is today or how many tasks call my name, please help me choose to sit at your feet and worship you. Help me choose the important and the eternal over the urgent and temporal.

The Lord answered her, "Martha, Martha,
you are worried and upset about many things.
Only one thing is important.
Mary has chosen the better thing,
and it will never be taken away from her."

—LUKE 10:41–42 NCV

Today I will not avoid looking at or addressing the real pain in this world.

FRIENDS WERE CONCERNED WHEN I was considering the offer to cohost the *700 Club* broadcasts, concerned that I would be burying my head in Christian television and sheltering myself from the real world. God had completely other plans for me, though. From the very first week I was on the program, I felt like God was throwing a bucket of ice water in my face every morning. I realized that, while I had thought I knew about needs and hurts, I didn't really know much at all. Now—and daily—I was dealing with people who had been brought up in desperate poverty, people caught in the trap of prostitution, drug addiction, child abuse, and myriad other human tragedies.

So when I heard a song on the radio—a song that at one time would have pulled me up out of drudgery and given me a boost of energy and hope—the lyrics didn't even come close to addressing what I was feeling and where I was hurting, especially the pain I was feeling for other people. After being on the *700 Club* for just a few weeks, I had a new sensitivity to what was happening in the world and how badly people needed a healing touch from Christ. I thought, *What have I been doing all this time? All these people are out there with real, open wounds, and so much of what I've done was like blowing up balloons and saying, "Let's have a party and all love Jesus!"*

When, if ever, have you realized just how much pain—and just how much pain beyond description—exists in this fallen world? What prompted that realization, and what did you do in response?

....

....

....

....

....

Think about the people in your life. Who might God want you to come alongside and help bear the burden of pain—or who do you think he is providing to help you bear the burden of your own pain? Act on his prompting.

....

....

....

....

....

The prayer of World Vision founder Bob Pierce is a scary prayer to pray, but it is a prayer of Christlikeness. Help me, Lord, to pray it with sincerity and an openness to how you'll use me in this world of hurting people: "May my heart be broken by the things that break the heart of God."

Bear one another's burdens, and so fulfill the law of Christ.

—GALATIANS 6:2

Today I will not avoid people who are hurting, facing death, or dealing with impossible circumstances.

I'VE ALREADY INTRODUCED YOU TO Debbie. I first met her back in 1989 when she called the *700 Club* and asked for me. A victim of the most debilitating form of multiple sclerosis, Debbie said, "I'm twenty-five, I'm dying of MS, and I'm scared. I love God, and I know I'm going to heaven. But I'm really scared, and you of all people should be the ones to help me. Why do you seem to be afraid to talk about death?" Well, I didn't have an answer for Debbie that day, and her question haunted me. The more I thought about it, the more I realized how easily we Christians can come across as saying, "How dare you not get well? We've prayed for you—and we've prayed some very good prayers! If you haven't gotten well, there must be something in your life that keeps you from being healed."

And as I prayed in the wake of Debbie's question, this image came to mind: "We as a church march along like a very triumphant, happy little band, and anytime members of our band fall down, we pick them up, dust them off, and say a quick prayer for them. If they recuperate, they continue marching along. If they don't, they fall behind, but we may not even know. We may never look back." And I imagined the Lord saying this: "I'm tired of coming along behind you to pick people up out of the gutter. That's really your job. It's time that you carried them. That's what the Christian walk is all about. If I choose to heal someone, I will. If not, I want that person to go from your arms to mine. Don't let hurting ones fall by the wayside and leave them there."

When has your pain or a tough situation seemed to prompt people—even believers—to avoid you? Why is that sometimes a reaction to a person's profound pain or loss?

....

....

Whose pain or loss has you feeling uneasy about coming alongside him or her? Why are you hesitant?

....

....

....

Lord, help me remember that coming alongside someone who is hurting and simply being there in silence can be a powerful expression of your love and a real source of comfort and hope. Remind me that I don't need to have the "right" words, but that if I do need to say something, you will provide the words for me. May I love with Christ's love those who especially need your touch this day.

Blessed be the God and Father of our Lord Jesus Christ, the Father of mercies and God of all comfort, who comforts us in all our tribulation, that we may be able to comfort those who are in any trouble, with the comfort with which we ourselves are comforted by God.

—2 CORINTHIANS 1:3–4

Today I will seek to share your grace with those I encounter.

LET ME INTRODUCE YOU TO some four-legged friends who have graced our life. Belle is a beautiful bichon frise who lives to please me. Tink is also a bichon frise, but she dances to the beat of "Wild Thing." And then there's Trevor, advertised as a Wiener dog but looking as if he is 10 percent Wiener and 90 percent Rottweiler—and my bichons gave Trevor the cold shoulder from the moment he came to live with us. They walked around him once or twice and then, with a shake of their perfectly groomed heads, left him in the dust. Yes, I have two bichon snobs.

Sometimes our brokenness can make us more like Belle and Tink than we care to acknowledge. There's something in us—sinners that we are—that wants to compare ourselves to others and say who gets to be "in" and who, like Trevor, is left out in the cold. God's boundless grace, though, has no room for prejudice. Every man, woman, and child is made and loved by God. He sees no distinction between shapes and sizes, races and colors, wealth and poverty, the cultured and the coarse. May I, today, share with everyone I meet the boundless grace of God, his grace that knows no limits!

When has someone—who was a little or a lot different from you—unexpectedly reached out to you? Talk about why you think that person did so and how you responded, internally and externally.

....

....

....

....

Think about those folks you can pretty much count on meeting today.
Who would benefit from a touch of God's grace as opposed to your
snobbish behavior—and what will you do to share that grace? Have a
couple of plans in mind.

....

....

....

....

*I'm ashamed to see how much like Belle and Tink I can be.
Please forgive me and help me to view others the way you see
them—as your precious and beloved creations. Please open
my heart today to the Trevors all around me, who need to
know the warmth of your grace and experience a touch of
your unconditional love.*

You are the light of the world. . . .
Let your light so shine before men,
that they may see your good works and
glorify your Father in heaven.
—Jesus in Matthew 5:14, 16

Today I will try to not take myself so seriously, knowing you love me in all my humanness.

I WAS SITTING IN MY salon, feeling quite pampered as someone worked on my fingernails and another on my feet. Settling into this moment of manicure/pedicure luxury, I was interrupted by a new employee who approached me and asked if I would like to have my eyebrows waxed. I politely declined because the last time I had that procedure done, it removed most of my forehead as well. This girl, with all the determination of a terrier, was not going to be left with idle hands! She continued in a loud voice, "How about your mustache? Can I wax your mustache?"

When I went home, I stared in the mirror and realized yet another gift from our compassionate God: as we age and things begin to grow on us, our eyesight begins to fade, too, so we remain blissfully unaware! And I thought of something else too. I could hardly wait to tell my close circle of friends with whom I share the triumphs and tragedies, the unexpected joys, and—in this case—the petty indignities of life. Solomon had it right: "Just as lotions and fragrance give sensual delight, a sweet friendship refreshes the soul" (Proverbs 27:9 MSG).

Think back on one of your most embarrassing moments. Were you able to laugh at yourself at least a little bit? Why or why not?

....

....

....

....

....

....

With what friends do you share life's triumphs, tragedies, joys, and indignities? Why do they increase the gladness and decrease the pain?

....

....

....

....

....

....

....

Lord God, the ability to laugh—especially the ability to laugh at ourselves—is a gift from you! A good belly laugh can be a mini-vacation in a day, a heart connection with a friend, and a perspective-giving gift of freedom! And laughter is richer when shared with friends. Thank you for both!

A merry heart makes a cheerful countenance.

—Proverbs 15:13

Today I will not beat myself up for my all-too-human stumbling, but rest in the love of you who hold me up.

HAVE YOU NOTICED THAT, WITHOUT the reality of his faithfulness and the power of God's love, we are powerless to live the kind of life he deserves from his people? If you're not convinced by the evidence in your own life, ask King David. He loved God—and committed adultery. He loved God—and was responsible for sending a man to certain death. . . . Look at Abraham, father of his people—and also a liar. He allowed another man to sleep with his wife, saying that Sarah was actually his sister. Look at Peter. He was privileged to walk side-by-side with Jesus day after day. He saw the miracles; he saw Lazarus raised from the dead. But when hard confrontation came, Peter said he'd never met Jesus. . . .

Human history is the ongoing story of both stumbling men and women *and* the constant grace and mercy of God. But consider this wonderful truth: God hits his target exactly, despite the fact he works with crooked arrows. The course of history—the history of salvation, the history of the world, and your own personal history—is all about him, never about us, never about the quality of the arrow. Yes, we need to do our best to live in ways that honor and glorify God, but we can also rest in the truth that he brings his good out of our sinfulness and stumbling.

Look at Romans 7:19 (on the following page). Which of your own traits and behaviors come to mind as you read Paul's words?

....

....

....

....

....

When have you experienced God using you, a crooked arrow, to do
something wonderful for his kingdom? Be specific—and let yourself be
encouraged!

....

....

....

....

....

*Lord, I do find it amazing that, after two thousand years, the
Christian faith is still around with us stumbling believers as
your advertisements! Thank you that you use us crooked arrows
for your right and perfect plans—but, Lord, help me cooperate
with your Spirit so I can fly straight and true!*

For the good that I will to do, I do not do;
but the evil I will not to do, that I practice.

—ROMANS 7:19

Today I will look for your light to shine into the dark moments and dark corners of my day.

THE SITUATION ON THE HOME front was bleak—relationally, spiritually, financially—yet God had clearly spoken to me before the darkness reached its darkest point. He had said, "I will deliver you." Believe me, I clung to that promise, but when the darkness became suffocatingly thick, my question became "So, exactly how will you do that?" I saw no sign of hope for getting out of the mess we were in.

But the more I spent time in my Father's presence, the more ridiculous my question seemed. The how didn't matter. All that mattered was *who*! If God my Father was telling me he would deliver me, then it didn't matter how or when. It was time for me to believe God can change any circumstance when we place our hope in him. My Father's message to me was clear: "Let go! Let go of trying to fix this. Let go of trying to work out what will happen. Let go of protecting yourself." I finally bowed my knee and let go. I released everything to God—my fear, my anger, my unforgiveness. I let go of all that and clung to my Father's hand.

When have you experienced hopelessness in your life? What do you do to combat despair?

....

....

....

....

....

....

....

What do you believe God is asking you to let go of? Will you let it go?

....

....

....

....

....

....

*Merciful and compassionate God, I bring to you every
situation where I have lost hope. . . . I ask for your grace,
your light, and your peace to be my comfort and guide.*

Then Jesus spoke to them again, saying, "I am the light
of the world. He who follows Me shall not walk in darkness,
but have the light of life."

—John 8:12

Today I will choose to believe that you will give me, just as you gave Peter, a new start on a limitless future in you.

"I DON'T KNOW THIS MAN!" With those words, the rough and tough Peter who was devoted to Christ took quite a fall. I am sure he beat himself up over the next few brutal hours and days as Jesus was crucified and placed in a tomb. How this betrayal must have weighed on Peter. He had denied so passionately that he would ever betray his Lord! Did Peter remember that Jesus had foretold this betrayal (Luke 22:31)—as well as his return? Jesus himself said to Peter, "Help your brothers be stronger when you come back to me" (v. 32 NCV). *When*, not *if*. And then there was the angel's message to the women at the empty tomb on that glorious Easter morning: "Go, tell [the risen Christ's] disciples—*and Peter*—that He is going before you into Galilee; there you will see Him, as He said to you" (Mark 16:7, emphasis added). God knew Peter's heart and knew that Peter needed the reassurance that he was still a disciple.

God knows your heart too. He knows which mess-ups you're concerned about. He knows that you wonder if he still hears you when you pray or cares about you when you stumble. He also knows the shame that arises when you consider facing what you have done and start walking the long path home. But hear this truth: with God, all things can be made new. Your past is just that, but your future in him is limitless. All God looks for is your desire to being moving in the right direction, and he will be there—and not just passively, but anxiously waiting to embrace you. You are loved; you are loved; you are loved!

What do you find especially encouraging in this snapshot from Peter's life?

....

....

....

What specific message of reassurance would you like to hear from the Lord?
Sit quietly with him, share your heart, and listen for his voice of love.

....

....

....

*Gracious and forgiving God, thank you for sharing Peter's
story in your Word. I need to see a confident follower . . .
humbled and broken . . . restored by your grace and for your
glory, as well as for the good of your kingdom. Help me, I pray,
like Peter, to let my past be in the past and to look to you for a
future in Jesus that is limitless. Here I am, Lord! Use me!*

I waited patiently for the LORD;
    And He inclined to me,
    And heard my cry.
He also brought me up out of a horrible pit,
    And set my feet upon a rock,
He has put a new song in my mouth—
    Praise to our God.

—PSALM 40:1–3

Today I will spend some time at the cross, in awe and gratitude for your truly amazing love.

"MY GOD, MY GOD, WHY have You forsaken Me?" (Matthew 27:46). Hear the agony in Jesus' words. It's unmistakable and heartbreaking. It's impossible for us to fathom how the Father and Son, united as they are in the mystery of the Trinity, were divided at that moment. Yet Jesus tasted the very essence of hell on our behalf: he experienced total separation from God. Yet in that moment was triumph, too, as Jesus once and for all took every sin, every ounce of shame and condemnation we will ever deserve, and embraced it. It was ordained that he would take our place under judgment, and with love he accepted that role. Such is his love, that he believed you and I are worth dying for.

The truth of Jesus' immeasurable love is truly beyond human understanding. Jesus believes that you and I are worth every flesh-ripping blow he took as he was flogged, every thorn that tore into his scalp, and every strike of the hammer against the nails that pierced his wrists. You are loved and valued more than you could ever hope or ask for. The greatest love story that Hollywood ever thought up could not hold a candle to the flame that burns in God's heart for you! Jesus took our shame on himself so you and I can enter our Father's presence as a child runs into the arms of the papa who loves her. The work of the cross that paid the price for our forgiveness, that covered the debt of our sin, is finished! We are free!

Although this account of Jesus' crucifixion is probably not new to you, what detail or statement gave you pause as you read it?

....

....

....

....

....

How does the story of Jesus' crucifixion continue to amaze and humble you today?

....

....

....

....

....

Loving Father, no words could ever begin to thank you for what Jesus did for me. That he would willingly endure such agony on behalf of wretched, unthankful sinners is beyond my comprehension. And how your heart must have ached over his pain and what my sin did to him. Please help me live the forgiven life in a way that honors you and brings you both glory!

[Jesus] said, "It is finished!"
And bowing His head, He gave up His spirit.
—JOHN 19:30

Today I will approach prayer as a gift that you give me.

MAYBE YOU'VE NEVER THOUGHT ABOUT it in quite this way, but do you realize that prayer is our lifeline between the physical world we can see and the spiritual world that is our eternal reality? That's one reason why prayer is essential to the Christian life: it focuses our vision and fine tunes our hearing so that we can come face to face with a God who can move not only mountains but our own hearts. But if prayer is key to our lives as believers, if it is such a powerful tool in God's hands to change us, why is prayer so hard to do? Four reasons are: not having time to pray, being too tired to pray, getting distracted, or not being sure that God is listening.

I totally understand those concerns and even empathize with them, yet I am convinced it would revolutionize our lives if we were better able to understand that prayer is a gift rather than a chore. Prayer is something to look forward to rather than something to be graded on. Prayer is our time to crawl into our Father's embrace and give our cares to him. It's not about how well we pray, but about *who* is listening to our prayers.

Which statement in this devotional challenges the way you have thought about prayer?

....

....

....

....

....

....

Which of the four reasons people don't pray do you struggle with most often? What might you do to overcome that particular barrier to prayer?

....

....

....

....

....

Lord God, forgive me when I forget that prayer is all about you. Prayer is time to worship and praise you, to be in your holy presence so that you may show me my sin, to thank you for the many blessings you pour into my life, and to lay before you concerns, always deferring to your will, to your good and perfect plan. Thank you for this privilege and amazing opportunity. May I not approach spending time with you as a chore or mere duty, but as a link to you who is my purpose, my joy, and eternal reality.

Rejoice always, pray without ceasing,
in everything give thanks; for this is the will of God
in Christ Jesus for you.

—1 THESSALONIANS 5:16–18

Today I will pray with confidence in your great trustworthiness.

SOME TIME AGO BARRY AND I did a very foolish thing. We bought a new house before our other house sold. I have counseled people against doing that very thing, but it's amazing how blind we can be when what we want is right in front of us. The new house had a nice yard for the dogs, and it was close to several of Christian's friends from school. So we put our house on the market, but it just sat there. The builder of the new house said there was quite a bit of interest in the home we really liked and if we wanted it, we should move on it. (Yes, I know: builders always say that.) Barry and I talked to someone at our bank, and we decided to go ahead. Surely the other house would sell in the summer! Yet summer came and went, as did fall. I felt sick that we had put ourselves in such a vulnerable position. I didn't even know how to pray. . . .

How could I ask God to help us sell a house when there were children dying of starvation around the world? How could I ask for help when it was our foolishness that had put us in this place? The answers to those questions are one and the same: I could then and always can ask God for help because he is a Father who welcomes me with open arms on the good days and the bad days of life. He is there for me to turn to when I make good choices and when I make bad ones. As the weeks passed, my assurance grew that, whatever happened in the real estate world, God was with us. Prayer forges within a deep awareness of God's trustworthiness.

What topics, if any, do you hesitate or even totally avoid talking to God about? Why—and what is the basis of that choice?

....

....

....

In what ways has prayer helped forge within you a deep awareness of
God's presence and trustworthiness?

....

....

....

*Holy and righteous God, it is amazing that you want sinners like
me to be in fellowship with you. Thank you for the privilege of
being your child—and please forgive this too-often disobedient
child for not always being open with you about mistakes and
poor choices, for avoiding certain topics in prayer, and even for
avoiding prayer altogether. Lord, I don't want the enemy to win!
Please make me a prayer warrior who, aware of your goodness
and trustworthiness, talks to you always and about everything.*

Whenever I am afraid,
I will trust in You.
In God (I will praise His word),
In God I have put my trust;
I will not fear.
What can flesh do to me?

—PSALM 56:3–4

Today I will ask with trust, expectation, and gratitude that you meet a specific need.

THE LOSS OF HER HUSBAND had been devastating. Of course emotionally, but also financially, yet she didn't want her children to worry. Buying clothing, however, was a struggle. Thankfully, the girls were well dressed due to the kindness of friends in her small church, but it was harder to dress her son. The church didn't have a lot of boys older or bigger than him, so the new pants he needed definitely created an opportunity for the family to see their heavenly Father provide for them. The four joined hands, and the mother prayed, "Father God, thank you for taking care of us. Thank you that you know what we need even before we ask. Even so, you have invited us to ask in Jesus' name. You know that we need pants, so I ask you to provide those—and I thank you in advance for your faithful provision."

The following evening the mother's friend dropped by for a cup of tea. When she left, she gave the mother a package. "I bought these for Tom, but he seems to have grown several inches overnight. These are far too short. Could your son wear them?" Inside the package the mother found three pairs of brand-new pants that fit her son perfectly. She was deeply grateful.

When has your heavenly Father surprised you or someone you know by meeting a specific need in an amazingly timely and fitting way? Be specific about the fingerprints of God that you saw on the situation.

....

....

....

....

....

Since your heavenly Father already knows what we need, why does he
invite us to ask him?

....

....

....

....

....

*Generous and gracious heavenly Father, I love stories like the one
I just read! You are so wonderful! Please help me remember this
special example of your faithfulness the next time—or maybe
right now—I need something. May I also remember that you,
who made a universe out of nothing, can certainly meet my needs.*

Your Father knows the things you have need
of before you ask Him.

—MATTHEW 6:8

Today I will pray with thanksgiving.

I HAVE VERY FEW HEROES. I'm not cynical about people, but I am fairly realistic about the fact that we believers are merely frail human beings, trying by the grace of God to be more like Jesus. I do have a few heroes, though—my mother being one and Ruth Bell Graham another. Ruth, now with the Lord, was a wise and gracious and godly woman who stood beside her famous husband for decades, touching lives in her own warm and significant way. One lesson she taught me was "Worship and worry cannot exist at the same time in the same heart. They are mutually exclusive." Let's look at that thought. . . .

We can pray and make our requests known to God, but we have to trust that God will answer our prayers. Thanksgiving helps us do that. When we pray with thanksgiving, we are saying that we believe the Lord will answer us, that he will provide for our needs or for the needs of those we love, and that we will be happy with his provision. Offering thanks helps us release our supposed control of the situation, acknowledge God's strength, and rejoice that he can take care of what we have brought before him. Giving thanks frees us from our worries and allows us rest. Besides, as a picture in Ruth's home said, "Edge your days with prayer; they are less likely to unravel." Especially if those prayers are thankful ones!

> When have you prayed with thanksgiving and, as a result, experienced the lifting of a burden and the peace that only God can give?
>
> ....
>
> ....
>
> ....

....

....

Concerned about one of her children, Ruth was unable to sleep one
night. Realizing the missing ingredient in her heart was thanksgiving,
she began to thank God for this son, for his life, for the joy he had
brought to their family. Her burden lifted, and she fell back asleep. What
current situation in your life is weighing you down? What aspects could
you genuinely thank God for?

....

....

....

....

*Teach me, Lord, to pray with thanksgiving—and, by doing
so, to declare my faith that you will answer, that you will
meet my needs, and that I will be content with your wise
and loving provision!*

Enter into His gates with thanksgiving,
    And into His courts with praise.
    Be thankful to Him, and bless His name.
For the LORD is good;
    His mercy is everlasting,
    And His truth endures to all generations.

—PSALM 100:4–5

Today I will remember that I don't have your big-picture perspective on those prayers that you have chosen not to answer as I would have liked you to.

IN 1872, GEOGRAPHER, EXPLORER, AND statistician Francis Galton conducted a research project to see if he could mathematically prove whether or not prayer works. His theory was simple: if prayer works, then the British royal family should live longer than any of their subjects, since they were prayed for regularly in churches and homes across the British Isles. However, when he compared the royal family's longevity with that of the general public, he found no difference. He therefore concluded that he had proven prayer does not work. (Galton did not, however, investigate the dietary habits or exercise regimens of Queen Victoria or Prince Albert!)

So how would Mr. Galton fit into today's world? Well, if you ask people in the United States if they believe in prayer, I think the majority of us would say that we do. The great divide would come when we started defining prayer, stating why we pray, and identifying who we believe we are praying to. Spend some time thinking about those three aspects as well as about specific evidence from your own life that prayer does work. But let's rephrase that! Think about the evidence in your own life that God does indeed answer the prayers of his people!

What is your definition of prayer? Why do you pray?

....

....

....

....

When have you seen evidence that God does indeed answer prayer—
sometimes in ways far greater than we could ask or imagine?

....

....

....

....

*Great and mysterious God, I am glad I don't have you
all figured out. You wouldn't be very big if I did! And I'm
thankful for the mystery of prayer, the mystery of partnering
with you in the unfolding of history—the history of the world,
of nations, of individuals, of loved ones. May I pray with
abundant faith in you who does indeed do far greater things
than we could ever ask or imagine.*

Now to Him who is able to do exceedingly abundantly above all
that we ask or think, according to the power that works in us,
to Him be glory in the church by Christ Jesus to all generations,
forever and ever. Amen.

—EPHESIANS 3:20–21

Today I will consider what it means that you are my Father.

WHEN MY DAD GAVE HIS heart to God later in life, he gave it all, and that was obvious in the very practical faith he lived out. If he saw someone with a real need, he did something about it. He didn't just pray; he was prepared to be the answer to his own prayers. He was spontaneous and a lot of fun. I thought he was wonderful . . . until a stroke changed him. Trapped in his crippled body, he never spoke a word. He moved about with a cane, and most of the time he seemed very weak. Then, as the months went by, my father went from being warm and gentle to being cold and unpredictable. His rage gave him the strength of three men, and later, realizing what he had done, he would hold his head in his hands and cry like a child.

It doesn't take a learned theologian to say which father I knew is most like our heavenly Father, but for years I was unable to pray to God the Father . . . and key to that was the tragedy of my earthly father. Yes, Scripture says that my heavenly Father knows what I need and will provide for me (Matthew 6:32). Jesus himself pointed out the important difference between earthly fathers and God: "If you then, being evil, know how to give good gifts to your children, how much more will your Father who is in heaven give good things to those who ask Him!" (Matthew 7:11). But only by God's redemptive power can I turn to him in total trust, fully relying on his patient, compassionate love—and it's available to you as well.

In what ways—positive and/or negative—has your relationship with your earthly father affected your relationship with your heavenly Father? Be specific.

....

....

....

....

Since becoming a believer, what has God done to show you his fatherly love for you? Give a few examples—and if they are hard to see, ask God's Spirit to open your heart and eyes so you can more easily recognize and more readily receive your heavenly Father's love.

....

....

....

....

*Lord God, you understand far more clearly than I do the ways
my relationship with my earthly father has, for good or bad,
impacted my relationship with you. . . . I simply ask that you
would help me, day by day, more freely receive your love and more
readily approach you, my perfect Father.*

Behold what manner of love
the Father has bestowed on us,
that we should be called children of God!

—1 JOHN 3:1

Today I will do all things for you and you alone, my audience of One.

WHY DOES GOD GIVE MORE gifts to some believers than others? Why do some Christians have much easier lives than others? Why does God say yes to some people's prayers and no to others? These are important questions to wrestle with. After all, since prayer is the most intimate form of communication between ourselves and God, if we believe God is favoring someone else over us, that sense will chip away at our trust and therefore at our prayer life.

Look again at those questions. Do you see how they are rooted in our looking around at others rather than living our life for the audience of One? We must keep in mind whom we're working for and serving—and that would be God himself and him alone. If we're dependent on the approval of others, life will be very discouraging. But if we wait only on the Lord, his love will uplift us no matter what. To God, there are no small jobs, menial tasks, or unimportant abilities. As far as I'm concerned, I work for God. He is my Boss and my King. So whether I am writing a book, recording a CD, speaking to twenty thousand women, or picking up the dry cleaning, it doesn't matter. No one thing that I am called to do is more important than another. All that matters is my heart.

What about this devotional do you find especially freeing?

....

....

....

....

....

....

Why do we find it hard to keep our focus on the truth that we are to serve God in all that we do—whether in the spotlight or behind the scenes?

....

....

....

....

....

....

Lord God, you know how hard it is for me to work to please you and you alone. The eyes of the crowd and its approval are so much more tangible. The world's "Well dones!" are so much easier to hear, and they come in such pleasurable forms, like money, status, prestige, stuff. Please forgive me when I play to the crowd instead of to you—and teach me to live, 24/7, for your glory . . . for you alone.

Whatever you do in word or deed,
do all in the name of the Lord Jesus, giving thanks
to God the Father through Him.

—COLOSSIANS 3:17

Today I will remember—by your grace—that you are right at my side always, enabling me to obey yet never leaving me even if I disobey.

FOR A LONG TIME IT was a puzzling scene. God didn't allow Moses to enter the Promised Land simply because he struck the rock twice?! Well, it's not that simple. In disobeying God and striking the rock twice, Moses blasphemed the picture of the coming Christ who would be struck once for us. Moses defiled a holy moment, so there was a price to be paid.

And as Moses paid that price for disobeying God, the Lord himself stayed right at the prophet's side. God took Moses to the top of the mountain and let him see the Promised Land. We don't know what took place there, but it seems to me a very intimate picture of a father lifting his son onto his shoulders to give him a better view. Then, when Moses died, God buried him (Deuteronomy 34:6). God took care of his friend and laid his body to rest. Even in his anger, God showed mercy and love toward Moses. Thankfully, God—who is the same yesterday, today, and tomorrow—extends the same gracious faithfulness to you and me that he extended to the great patriarch Moses. We disobey, yet God stays at our side.

What did you learn about Moses and/or God in today's devotional?

....

....

....

....

....

....

When during a season of your own disobedience were you aware of God's presence with you?

....

....

....

....

....

....

Faithful and just God, you alone could perfectly balance those two qualities in your dealing with us. Thank you that you do so—and thank you that you are with us always as the consequences of our sin plays out in our life.

Christ also suffered *once* for sins,
the just for the unjust, that He might bring
us to God, being put to death in the flesh
but made alive by the Spirit.
—1 PETER 3:18 (EMPHASIS ADDED)

Today I will choose to trust you and pray to you even if you seem far away and unhearing.

WE CHRISTIANS CAN'T HELP BUT be a bit in awe of Job, whose life God gave Satan permission to tear apart. Job lost everything. His sons, daughters, and servants were killed, and his vast herds of livestock were stolen. Tragedy visited Job on every level. At one point Job said, "Though he slay me, yet will I trust him" (Job 13:15). Yet at another point, the very human Job said this: "I cry out to you, God, but you do not answer; I stand up, but you just look at me. You have turned on me without mercy" (30:20–21 NCV). Job wanted to trust God, but his life situation seemed so unfair. That's when Elihu, though a young man, offered some wise advice. . . .

Read carefully what Elihu said: "Watch out! . . . Don't let your suffering embitter you at the only one who can deliver you" (36:18 TLB). God truly is the only One who can deliver us from whatever circumstances, uncertainty, loss, challenges, or pain we are dealing with, and we must choose to trust him. No matter what happens, no matter how inexplicable life can be, we must trust God rather than give in to despair. We must choose to believe that God is faithful even when he seems far away.

Why do you think God is sometimes silent in our times of suffering?

....

....

....

....

....

What do you appreciate about Elihu's statement? Is it helpful? Why or
why not?

....

....

....

....

....

Lord, it's hard to choose to trust you when you seem far away.
It's hard to keep praying when you don't seem to be hearing.
But help me to take those simple steps of faith and keep
believing with my whole heart that you hear every word.

Then Job arose, tore his robe, and shaved his head; and he fell to the
ground and worshiped. And he said:
"Naked I came from my mother's womb,
And naked shall I return there.
The LORD gave, and the LORD has taken away;
Blessed be the name of the LORD."
In all this Job did not sin nor charge God with wrong.

—JOB 1:20–22

Today I will ask you whatever question comes to mind.

TO QUESTION GOD IS NOT to lack faith. I am confident that we can trust God and still ask questions. In fact, asking questions is simply evidence that we are being honest with him. And I believe God wants us to be honest because he wants a real relationship with us, not something fake or half-hearted. I believe he wants us to come before him and say, "God, this makes no sense to me. I hurt so badly. I just don't understand—and I probably never will—but I love you and trust you. And I rest in the fact that you know how I feel. You've had your heart ripped out. So even though I can't understand what is happening to me, help me glorify you through it."

Imagine being God and loving us, his children, with a passion so great that you gave your only Son to hang on a cross and be ripped in two. How must it feel to have that kind of love as the very essence of your being and yet, day after day, have your hurting children come to you but only say, "Well, thank you for another day"! They never open up. They—some of us—are never honest. How that must grieve God's heart!

What questions, if any, have you never asked God? Why?

....

....

....

....

....

....

What do you appreciate about the picture of God presented in today's devotional? Spend some time praising your heavenly Father.

....

....

....

....

....

....

....

Lord God, Heavenly Father, Friend of sinners, thank you that I can be totally honest with you. Thank you that you want a genuine relationship with me, one void of pretense and one in which any topic is invited. May I always come before you with openness and honesty, editing neither thoughts, questions, or emotions.

Be anxious for nothing, but in everything
by prayer and supplication, with thanksgiving,
let your requests be made known to God.

—PHILIPPIANS 4:6

Today I will walk humbly and gratefully with you, my Lord.

WHEN JESUS REDEEMS YOUR LIFE, it is changed forever. Now understand something about that truth that I haven't always known: a life redeemed by God doesn't necessarily mean that all your external circumstances change, but because the risen Christ is present with you and in you, your life is full of purpose and hope. Yes, I used to think that when you love and follow Christ, he would change those life circumstances that are painful or clear your path of potential potholes. I believe now that the truth is far greater: rather than get us or keep us out of trouble, Jesus lives in us through any troubles we encounter.

Consider that, after the death and resurrection of Christ, Pilate was still in power, Herod still ruled, and the Roman soldiers still rode their horses through the streets of Jerusalem. Nothing had changed in the world of politics—but, in a very real way, everything had changed. After all, sin had been crucified and death had been defeated. Likewise, your world probably didn't turn right-side up when you accepted Jesus as your Savior and Lord. When we look only at external circumstances, we are in danger of missing the whole point of the miracle and gift we have been given. Yet, when you know that the God who holds the universe in place, and who knows all that is true about you, loves you enough to die for you, how could your life ever be meaningless again?

What contributes to those moments when life seems meaningless? Be sure to manage those contributing factors that you can control (time with the Lord, sleep, exercise, diet, balance, busyness, etc.), so that you aren't an easy target for the enemy's lies.

....

....

....

....

In what ways was everything about your world different once you
accepted Jesus as your Savior and Lord?

....

....

....

....

*God of wonders, it is a wonder that you chose me to be your
child. Thank you for that amazing grace and for the purpose
and meaning with which you and your love fill my life. May I
live in a way that honors and glorifies you—and makes others
notice and want to know you too.*

He has shown you, O man, what is good;
   And what does the LORD require of you
   But to do justly,
   To love mercy,
   And to walk humbly with your God?

—MICAH 6:8

Today I will give you all I have to use as you will.

REMEMBER THE LITTLE BOY WHO probably got too busy on the playground during lunch to eat what his mom had lovingly packed for him? On the way home, he came across a huge crowd and a man asking if anyone had any food. The boy handed over his five little loaves and two fish, and the rest—as they say—is history! In fact, the event is reported and the boy is given credit in John 6:9, but the miracle is recorded in Matthew 14, Mark 6, and Luke 9 as well.

What we actually know of this boy's story is pretty bare bones: he gave what he had to Jesus. Yet we see that, in return, he was blessed to witness what God can do when heaven and earth hold hands. Everyone who believes in Jesus is invited to participate in exactly that kind of a miracle: each of us is invited to bring all we have to the Lord God and then see what he will do! Too often, though, when we daughters of the King look at what we have to offer, it hardly seems enough, and we hold back. Whatever you have today *is* enough. It might not look like it to you, but when you put into Jesus' hands, it is more than enough.

When have you given something to Jesus and seen him make it more than enough?

....

....

....

....

....

....

....

What has God been asking you to give him? Be specific. Also, consider why you may have hesitated or be hesitating to hand it over.

....

....

....

....

....

....

....

Father God, today I bring my life to you as an offering. I ask that you would do what only you can do as I watch heaven touch earth.

Another of his disciples, Andrew,
Simon Peter's brother, spoke up,
"Here is a boy with five small barley loaves
and two small fish,
but how far will they go among so many?"

—JOHN 6:8–9 NIV

Today I will invest myself in a friendship with a fellow believer, either by reaching out or opening up to a brother or sister in Christ.

"Hello. I'm Sheila, and I'm a sinner. I need your help." Can you imagine what freedom would come to the body of Christ if each of us would stand up and say that? After all, any apparent perfection we show fellow believers creates a gulf between us and them, but being open about our brokenness builds a bridge. It's hard to admit helplessness over our behavior and ask for help, but I don't want to be enchained by pride and fear. I want to find healing. I want to share life with fellow believers. I want to live with real people, and I want to be real too.

Admitting our need—admitting that we need help to quit being victims or abusers or addicts or hypocrites—can free us as well as the generations to come. Confessing to a fellow believer why I walk with a limp or the reason I have scars—telling a brother or sister in Christ about my journey through life—is what God desires for me. He longs for us to reach out to one another as fellow travelers on this treacherous journey called life.

When have you felt the need to put on that Cheshire-cat grin among believers? What prompts us to feel that pressure? What compels us to comply?

....

....

....

....

What fellow traveler has reached out to you and accepted the truth-telling you offered? What was the impact of this Christlike love and acceptance?

....

....

....

....

I thank you for the ways you have made your love for me real through your people. May I be that kind of friend to someone today. Show me who needs a listening ear—and empower me to be their friend.

Two are better than one,
Because they have a good reward for their labor.
For if they fall, one will lift up his companion.
But woe to him who is alone when he falls,
For he has no one to help him up.

—ECCLESIASTES 4:9–10

Today I will practice praying for your will to be done in whatever situation I lay before you.

"ASK ANYTHING IN MY NAME, Sheila—and I'll do it for you!" That's my paraphrase of a great but very misunderstood promise in Scripture. At one point, however, I thought it meant I could pray to be four inches taller. (I maxed out at five foot four, a fact that made me very unhappy when I was sixteen.) And I *could* pray that, but I have since learned that when we take what we want and try to twist God's arm to answer us ("If I am two inches taller in the morning, I'll be a missionary!"), we have shifted from worshipers to spoiled children. We are saying essentially, *Here is what I want, Father. I am asking in Jesus' name so you have to give it to me.*

So can we ask God for anything if our faith is strong enough? Well, yes— but is that really the right question? Prayer—or, more specifically, answered prayer—is not so much about our level of faith as it is what we put our faith in. Are we asking for the right things? Are we seeking God's will in the situation? Are we comfortable with his response if things don't end up the way we want? Also, consider that Jesus lived every moment of his time on earth to serve his heavenly Father and bring the King of kings glory. Looking at that fact and longing to be like Jesus are changing the way I pray, and they may change your praying. So let's keep pouring our hearts out to God, but may our daily cry be what Jesus' was: "But, please, not what I want, Father. What do you want?"

When, if ever, have you seen God change your heart over time as you persevered in bringing a certain prayer request before him?

....

....

....

....

What is your answer to the question "Can we ask God for anything"?

....

....

....

Loving and patient God, thank you for accepting me in all my humanness, a humanness that is often revealed in my prayers. Thank you for this day's reminder to keep your big-picture perspective in mind (will what I'm requesting further your kingdom?) and to pray according to your will (not my will, but thine be done). And continue to teach me, I pray, about the powerful, wonderful mystery of prayer.

I tell you the truth, anyone who believes in me
will do the same works I have done, and even greater works,
because I am going to be with the Father.
You can ask for anything in my name, and I will do it,
so that the Son can bring glory to the Father.
Yes, ask me for anything in my name, and I will do it!

—JESUS IN JOHN 14:12–14 NLT

Today I will walk with you so that I can know you better and trust you more—and more easily.

HAVE YOU BEEN SO HURT by someone that you've found yourself asking, "Where were you, God?" about that painful situation. If so, you know it can be very difficult to trust people again. Heartbreakingly, you may also find it hard to trust God again; you may withdraw from the only One who can truly make things right. Blindly pulling away from him serves no purpose but harm. God would rather we come to him and tell him we're having trouble with faith than not come to him at all. In fact, God promises that if we trust him and don't try to figure things out for ourselves, he will lead us toward faith. He knows we won't always understand the why of things, but he tells us that even if we can't trust others, we can trust him.

If we simply trust God, with no strings attached, wonderful things can happen. I'm not saying we won't live through trials, but children learn to trust their parents even though their childhood is not pain-free. Think of the mom who takes her child to the doctor for an injection. Standing there with her young son, she might wonder if he'll trust her again—but once the shot has been administered, he reaches to her for comfort. That surely is a picture of the trust our Father longs for us to know. Furthermore, we who are children of God are not to tie our trust to whether God acts the way we want him to act. If we do so, we will be disappointed. But if we realize that a straight path—a path straight to where God wants us to go—doesn't necessarily mean a path without bumps or curves, and if we spend time getting to know better the One we are being asked to trust, we can find trust coming more easily. I've reached that point—I may not always like where God takes me, but if it's where he's going, then I'm going too—and I pray you will too.

Why do you find it hard to trust God?

....

....

....

What trial of yours has actually helped you trust your heavenly Father more? Describe that experience.

....

....

....

> *Father, today I place my hand in your hand. Wherever you are going, I'm coming with you. I won't always understand the path or the whys, but I trust your heart. I trust your love. And help me, I pray, to grow in trust.*

Trust in the LORD, and do good;
    Dwell in the land, and feed on His faithfulness. . . .
Commit your way to the LORD,
    Trust also in Him.

—PSALM 37:3, 5

Today I will remind myself that you are sovereignly creating from my life a work much more beautiful than I can imagine.

MAYBE YOU'VE HEARD THIS STORY about Corrie ten Boom. When she spoke about her horrifying experience in a Nazi concentration camp and God's grace in the midst of such cruelty and squalor, she would hold up the wrong side of a tapestry for her audience to see. "Isn't it beautiful?" she would ask—but no one would agree. Looking at the back of the tapestry, the people saw only threads crossed at odd intervals, knotted in places, looking clumsy and disjointed. It was, to be blunt, actually quite ugly. The audience sat quietly, not knowing how to respond to Corrie's question. After a few seconds of silence, Corrie would say, "Oh! Yes, of course! You can't see the tapestry from my perspective." Then Corrie would turn the piece of cloth around to show the front, and there would be a picture of a beautiful crown.

At times, life makes no sense. It is disjointed, distorted, and ugly. The threads are crossed at odd intervals, and the number of knots is dizzying and hardly attractive. But if we surrender our view of the back side of life for God's not-yet-seen but much grander picture—a design that reflects order, intentionality, and beauty—we will always be better able to hold on to our eternal hope in Christ Jesus.

When has God graciously given you a glimpse of the beautiful picture he is creating on the other side of the knots and crossed threads of your life?

....

....

....

What tangles in your life can only be made beautiful by God's divine intervention? May the Lord use the specifics of that incident you just recalled to fuel your hope about the beauty he will bring from today's tangles.

....

....

....

Gracious Creator God, you know how easily I see the knots and tangles of life and how easily I let go of the truth I know in my head: these are real afflictions, but they are light and temporary, and you are using them to create a life-picture that will give you glory. I believe; help my unbelief.

We do not lose heart. . . . For our light affliction, which is but for a moment, is working for us a far more exceeding and eternal weight of glory, while we do not look at the things which are seen, but at the things which are not seen. For the things which are seen are temporary, but the things which are not seen are eternal.

—2 CORINTHIANS 4:16–18

Today I will, at each decision point and by your grace, remember that my actions make a difference to you and ask you to help me choose wisely.

HERE'S A MIND-BOGGLING THOUGHT: YOUR life and your actions make a difference to God. Want some evidence? I offer the first and last chapters of Job. Writer Phillip Yancey says that the "wager" between God and Satan—Satan's accusation that Job would turn from God if God withdrew all the blessings—"resolved decisively that the faith of a single human being counts for very much, indeed."* To think otherwise is to fall into Satan's trap and believe that our lives and our actions don't really make a difference. Satan loves it when the Christian sales rep who struggles with pornography reaches one more time for the adult television channel while alone in his hotel room. The devil rejoices when the young woman who, tired of her marriage, lies in her husband's arms and dreams of someone else.

Life can be hard—and grossly unfair. When the bad things happen, we often ask, "Can I trust God?" But perhaps the real question is "Can God trust me?" Can he trust you and me to hold on? Can he trust us to want to become mature Christians, or will we remain little children who believe in him only if he makes it worth our while? When life seems to cave in for no reason, will we remember that God is faithful? Will you?

What was your initial reaction to the statement that "your life and your actions make a difference to God"? Comment on the evidence Phillip Yancey offers. Are you convinced? Why or why not?

....

....

....

Can God trust you to hold on to your faith in him when—not *if*—life caves in? Remember too that he is holding you!

....

....

....

> *Trustworthy God, when life next caves in—and it will in this sin-ravaged world—I pray that you will find me trustworthy, that you will find me remembering that you are faithful and trusting you to bring me through circumstances I don't like or understand.*

Be strong and of good courage, do not fear nor be afraid of them; for the LORD your God, He is the One who goes with you. He will not leave you nor forsake you.

—DEUTERONOMY 31:6

---

* Phillip Yancey, *Disappointment with God* (Grand Rapids: Zondervan, 1988), 170.

Today I will find a way to be an unexpected source of encouragement to someone.

ON A TRIP TO NEW York City, I had the opportunity to attend the Brooklyn Tabernacle, pastored by Jim Cymbala. I was scheduled to provide some special music for the service, and I was happy to do so. As I always do before a concert or church service where I'm singing, I arrived in plenty of time to do a sound check in peace and quiet before the crowd came in. What I didn't know was that at Brooklyn Tabernacle, the worshipers come in before anything begins. People were everywhere, yelling at me, asking who I was, hugging me—but I was determined to do my sound check it if killed me, and it looked like it just might! One nail went in the coffin when we played the first tape through the machine, and it was awful. "I can't sing to this," I wailed. "I can't even hear it! It's terrible!" Then, when I tried to sing through the microphone, it sounded as if I were strangling a large cat. I had to get out of there!

Having made it outside, I was standing and talking to God when I felt someone put a hand into my hand and squeeze tightly. I looked down, and there was a little girl. She was probably twelve years old. As I looked into her eyes, she grinned one of those grins that stretches from ear to ear, and she said, "Isn't it great to know that Jesus loves us?"

When has God offered some special and especially meaningful encouragement through an unexpected source? Enjoy the moment again as you describe it in detail.

....

....

....

....

....

For whom will you be an unexpected source of encouragement today? If no one comes to mind right away, how about sending—anonymously—a note of appreciation to a pastor or Bible study leader?

....

....

....

....

....

> *Gracious God, I thank you for the times your people have encouraged me with warm words and kind gestures. Forgive me when, in my busyness and self-centeredness, I miss opportunities to do so for others. Help today be different—and every tomorrow after that!*

Be joyful. Grow to maturity. Encourage each other. Live in harmony and peace. Then the God of love and peace will be with you.

—2 Corinthians 13:11 NLT

Today I will remember that— whatever the headlines are, whatever suffering I encounter, whatever challenges I or loved ones face—it is well with my soul.

REMEMBER THAT ROUGH BEGINNING TO my appearance at Brooklyn Tabernacle? God intervened so tenderly when, after a rough (to say the least) sound check, he sent a little girl to remind me: "Isn't it great to know that Jesus loves us?" Well, that wasn't the last I saw of God's intervention that morning. As I sang my first two songs, I realized I was not reaching the hearts of the precious people who had come to worship the Lord. My songs were nice enough; the words were solid. But these words weren't reaching the people, especially those who were living in desperate situations and knew the harsh realities of New York City street life. So I stopped in the middle of my presentation and asked for a hymnbook.

"When peace, like a river, attendeth my way / When sorrows like sea billows roll; / Whatever my lot, Thou hast taught me to say, / 'It is well, it is well with my soul.'"* By God's grace, these words touched the hearts of people who needed to know his love and strength. That hymn, written by a man who lost his four daughters and all his possessions in a terrible shipwreck, reminds us that whatever we face, whatever we go through, we can still embrace the solid truth that, because of the Cross, "It is well, it is well with my soul."

When has the truth that "it is well with [your] soul" enabled you to keep putting one foot in front of the other?

....

....

....

....

What current circumstances in your life does this truth put in perspective for you, the perspective of eternity, the perspective that your sovereign God is on the throne?

....

....

....

....

Almighty God, you know the ways in which my life feels shipwrecked. Thank you for today's reminder that, despite the circumstances I wish were different, "it is well with my soul."

If God is for us, who can be against us?
—ROMANS 8:31

---

* These words are from "It Is Well with My Soul" by Horatio G. Spafford, 1828–1888, altered.

Sheila Walsh wants every little girl to know she is the daughter of the King!

Make sure your little princess grows up in the knowledge of this love with the bestselling God's Little Princess Devotional Bibles.

Prayers, Scripture, Activities, and more to engage and entertain her as she discovers her destiny as His.

Beautiful Things Happen

WHEN A
WOMAN
TRUSTS
GOD

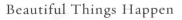

SHEILA WALSH

Delivering a big message with strong Biblical insights and heartening personal stories, bestselling author, Sheila Walsh shows women the life-changing power of trusting in God.